BUS

Why the Markets went Crazy

Also by Tim Lee

Economics for Professional Investors

WHY THE MARKETS WENT CRAZY

And What it Means for Investors

Tim Lee

First published 2004 by
PALGRAVE MACMILLAN
Houndmills, Basingstoke, Hampshire RG21 6XS and
175 Fifth Avenue, New York, N.Y. 10010
Companies and representatives throughout the world

PALGRAVE MACMILLAN is the global academic imprint of the Palgrave
Macmillan division of St. Martin's Press, LLC and of Palgrave Macmillan Ltd.
Macmillan® is a registered trademark in the United States, United Kingdom
and other countries. Palgrave is a registered trademark in the European
Union and other countries.

ISBN 1–4039–1869–4

This book is printed on paper suitable for recycling and made from fully
managed and sustained forest sources.

A catalogue record for this book is available from the British Library

Library of Congress Cataloging-in-Publication Data

Lee, Tim, 1959–

    Why the markets went crazy : and what it means for investors / Tim Lee.
      p. cm.
    Includes bibliographical references and index.
    ISBN 1–4039–1869–4
     1. Stock Market Bubble, 1995–2000. 2. Stock exchanges. 3. Financial crises.
   4. Investments. 5. Stock exchanges—United States. 6. Financial crises—United
   States. 7. Investments—United States. I. Title.

HG4551.L347 2003
338.5'42—dc22

2003053699

10 9 8 7 6 5 4 3 2 1
13 12 11 10 09 08 07 06 05 04

Printed and bound in Great Britain by
Creative Print & Design (Wales), Ebbw Vale

Contents

List of Figures

Preface and Acknowledgements

This book is about the greatest financial mania that the world has ever seen. It is a story that is still unfolding, and therefore will no doubt be much better understood in the future. However, I take the view that, certainly from the point of view of investors, the more that is understood now about the economic and financial events of recent years the better.

At the risk of seeming arrogant, it seems to me, writing this in early March 2003, that many who are involved in financial markets (not all) still have much to understand about the nature of financial developments in the 1990s, and the nature of the fallout from those excesses. (At the time of writing this preface the focus of market comment was exclusively on the likelihood of the 2003 war against Iraq.) A Rip Van Winkle, waking from three years of sleep and turning to the financial media, could be forgiven for assuming that the whole three-year global bear market in equities has been attributable to this imminent war. Some prominent market strategists – including one or two in that minority that still retain a reserve of credibility – are talking of an 'important bottom' being made in the markets, with the prospect of a resumption of strong returns from equities once the war uncertainty is out of the way. They would do well to read again the words penned (in the admittedly ultimately different circumstances of the 1930s) by Graham and Dodd, quoted in the final chapter of this book.

With this overall theme as the background, I have tried to achieve three things with this book: first, to convince the reader of the scale of the 1990s mania, partly with some reminders of the financial developments of that time; second, to provide an analysis of what happened, and is happening; third, to draw a few conclusions for the future from that analysis with, of course, the usual caveats about the lack of certainty that always underlies economic and financial forecasting. The analysis is concentrated in Chapters 3, 4 and 5. Those without any background in economics or finance might find parts of these chapters a little difficult to follow (although there is no use of mathematics). I would like to reassure any such readers that a complete understanding of everything in these chapters is not necessary for following the broad themes and conclusions of the book. Conversely, those readers with a background in economics and finance might be dissatisfied that I have not used reams of statistics to back up the arguments I advance.

This reflects my personal prejudice that economic statistics can be as misleading as they are useful, and they are no substitute for principles. A subtheme of the book, particularly in Chapter 6, is that excessive attention to statistical methods was an enabling factor in the equity mania.

I wrote *Why the Markets went Crazy* on an almost full-time basis between August 2002 and the beginning of 2003. The book is therefore based on information and data available up to the end of 2002. I would like to thank my family, Hilda, Jamie and Caroline, for their support. I would, in particular, like to thank my wife Hilda for her suggestions for alterations that have made the book more readable. While I have been writing the book over this period I have relied upon a number of contacts to help keep me in touch with the ongoing developments in financial markets. I am grateful to Matthew Lonergan, Simon Ogus and to the economists at Dresdner Kleinwort Wasserstein, Credit Suisse First Boston and HSBC Investment Bank for their help in this respect.

Special thanks go to my literary agent, Liz Puttick, of Elizabeth Puttick Literary Agency, for her assistance, and particularly for finding, in Palgrave Macmillan, such an excellent publisher for this book. I am very grateful to Professor Steve H. Hanke and to Roger Yates for their comments on the manuscript and synopsis.

I alone of course take sole responsibility for the views I have expressed, but I must acknowledge that I owe much inspiration to a number of excellent financial economists whom it has been my privilege to work with over the years. I would particularly like to mention John Greenwood and Jonathan Mann, who introduced me to a number of the concepts and ideas that I have made use of here. I am also indebted to other former economists of GT Management, an asset management company that, sadly and to the loss of the world of investment, no longer exists, at least in part because its more 'traditional' approach to equity investment ultimately did not survive the mania that emerged progressively during the 1980s and 1990s. In particular, I owe much to Hugh Sloane, Daniel Gressel and Ian Macfarlane.

The book makes use of a number of quotes from authoritative sources to lend support to arguments that I have advanced in the book. I would like to note my thanks to McGraw-Hill for granting me permission to reproduce the excerpt from Graham and Dodd's 1934 classic *Security Analysis*. I would also like to thank John Wiley & Sons for permission to use a quote from Charles Kindleberger's *Manias, Panics, and Crashes*. I am particularly indebted to investment bank Morgan Stanley and also to Dr Henry Kaufman for their kind permissions to quote brief extracts from research articles. The *Financial Times* has given permission for the use of a small number of short extracts from articles published in the newspaper, which have also been used to lend authority to points of view I have expressed. These more substantive quotes are fully referenced in the list of references at the back of the book. For less significant quotes and extracts I have included references to sources within the text. Where I have quoted comments made by officials, reported in the news media, or in cases where it is more appropriate to preserve the anonymity of the writer or speaker, I have not given a full reference.

March 2003 **Tim Lee**

CHAPTER I

Introduction: The 1990s Financial Mania in Perspective

It is tempting to view the 1990s stock market bubble and its aftermath in the same light as previous episodes of mania and panic in financial history. It is my contention in this book that to take this view entirely would be a mistake; that both quantitatively and qualitatively the 1990s stock market bubble was a unique occurrence, the ramifications of which will be felt for a long time and the consequences of which will ultimately prove very different from those that are widely expected or feared. The uniqueness of this most recent boom and bust can be summarized in four points, which I explore and support in this book:

1. The 1990s financial bubble is usually referred to as the 'internet bubble', 'high-tech bubble' or 'TMT (technology, media and telecommunications) bubble' but it was actually much broader in scope and duration than any of these descriptions imply, incorporating much more of the global stock market, and also the bond markets. In terms of the apparent increase in wealth (that is financial market capitalization) it far surpassed any previous experience. Simply put, it was the greatest financial mania in history.

2. Although previous financial manias have generally had an international dimension, this was the first truly 'global bubble' in that it affected all financial markets in all regions of the globe.

3. The financial mania was so large and long-lasting that its economic effects have been far more pervasive than in a typical 'cyclical' experience. The mania has had significant consequences for the structure of the global economy, and therefore can be considered to have been a 'structural bubble'.

4. Unlike most previous bubbles, the bursting of the bubble has not been consequent upon severely tighter liquidity or monetary conditions. On

the contrary, the world's monetary authorities acted aggressively, and largely pre-emptively, to forestall the effects of the bubble burst, slashing interest rates to multi-decade lows. Central bank action was quantitatively different from that in previous episodes in history, and this is important to the understanding of the long-term likely outcomes.

The book would not be complete without a brief review of some of the extraordinary excesses of the internet mania, but it is not my main intention to add to the considerable amount that has already been written on this subject. Rather, my aim is to provide an analysis of the behaviour of the financial markets as a whole over the past few years, which I believe provides key insights into the nature of the financial bubble and, most importantly, pointers to the economic risks that face us all in the future.

Financial manias and panics in themselves are nothing new. They have occurred regularly throughout economic history and there is a respectable volume of literature on the subject, the most well-known contribution to which is probably Charles P. Kindleberger's classic book *Manias, Panics, and Crashes: A History of Financial Crises*. The typical characteristics of mania and subsequent crash described by Kindleberger can be seen clearly in the late 1990s bubble in technology, media and telecommunication (TMT) shares. To quote selectively from the fourth edition of Kindleberger's book:

> 'some event changes the economic outlook. New opportunities for profits are seized, and overdone, in ways so closely resembling irrationality as to constitute a mania. Once the excessive character of the upswing is realized, the financial system experiences a sort of "distress" . . . it happens that crashes and panics often are precipitated by the revelation of some misfeasance, malfeasance, or malversation (the corruption of officials) engendered during the mania. It seems clear . . . that swindles are a response to the greedy appetite for wealth stimulated by the boom.'[1]

These quotes might serve as good a summary as any of the TMT bubble and burst.

Despite their indisputable existence, in conventional, classical, economics there is no real place for bubbles or manias. In classical economic theory individuals' preferences are assumed to be independent of each other and expectations about the future reflect all available information and are not directly influenced by one-off changes in price levels. These assumptions are necessary to prove that free markets will produce an 'equilibrium' that is stable and represents an optimal position for the economy. So, for instance, if the price of a share or currency were to fall while all other observable factors remained unchanged then that share or currency would become more attractive to investors because it would be cheaper. Conversely, if it were to rise it would be more expensive and so less attractive a proposition. In this type of world financial manias cannot exist. A bubble or mania can be thought of, simply, as a situation in which price increases for a particular asset or class of assets cause demand for the asset to increase and beget further price increases because investors are influenced by each other's behaviour and the recent behaviour of prices themselves.

Kindleberger explains that every mania differs in some way from previous manias. There is a new object of speculation, a justification for price appreciation that is difficult to deny. In the 1970s various commodities were 'running out'. In the 1980s the Japanese economic model was unbeatable and Japan and Asia were set completely to dominate the world in the present century. In the late 1990s the internet and advances in telecommunications were completely changing the way consumers and businesses would operate, making possible new and vastly more efficient business models. Or so it all seemed at the time.

Modern ideas in behavioural economics and finance dispute the assumptions of classical economics and allow for the possibility of manias and panics. In his book *Butterfly Economics*[2] Paul Ormerod describes an experiment in which two identical food sources were placed at an equal distance from a nest of ants and were constantly replenished to ensure they remained identical. After the experiment had been running for a while it was observed that the proportion of ants visiting any one site could oscillate in large, random, swings. At one time 80 per cent of the ants might be visiting one of the two sites and this proportion might remain stable for a while but in the end this majority would be eroded and the ants would switch, sometimes rapidly, to visiting the other site. Ormerod argues that this is the result that should be expected if each individual ant retains some capacity for independent action, but exhibits some inertia in having a tendency to repeat past actions, and furthermore can also be influenced by the behaviour of other ants. He argues that the individuals and companies that make up the economy behave in a similar way to the ants, with the result that the economy and financial markets are susceptible to 'feedback' effects.

Closely related to Ormerod's 'ants model' is the concept of 'reflexivity' described by legendary investor George Soros in his book *The Alchemy of Finance*.[3] Soros's reflexivity is the interaction between market participants' expectations and outcomes, such that expectations influence outcomes as well as outcomes influencing expectations. As with the ants, market participants' expectations and actions are not formed and taken independently of one another's. Furthermore, expectations held in any one market are continually changing in response to price changes in other markets that are themselves the result of shifting expectations.

In this type of 'reflexive' model there are potentially large 'feedback' effects that mean that there is no tendency to a stable equilibrium position as there is in classical economics. Consider this hypothetical example, relating to the stock market: two successive months of economic data give the impression of a possible improvement in economic activity after a period of weakness. In fact the data are merely affected by random statistical noise but market participants do not know this. They respond to the data by pricing into markets the possibility that the economy may be beginning an upturn. Stock prices rise and bond markets fall, meaning higher bond yields, interpreted by some as meaning a slightly greater risk of inflation in the future. Some businesses respond to these signals by accumulating inventories, increasing the demand seen by other sectors of the economy. As a result certain commodity prices rise a little and businesses register higher levels of confidence as measured in the various surveys of business confidence. Financial markets see the stronger readings of business confidence and the move up in commodity prices as confirmation of an economic upturn under way, pricing in a greater certainty of a pick-up in the shape of a further rise in bond yields and stock prices, in turn giving greater impetus to rising business confidence and inventory accumulation. Once started the cycle goes on, spreading to business investment and employment and consumption as the expansion goes forward, an expansion which, in this example, owes itself initially to randomness in the economic statistics being interpreted by the markets.

A friend, and ex-colleague, once asked me the following, almost philosophical, question: 'If rogue statisticians in the government's statistics department were making up some of the economic data, would the markets behave as if the statistics were the truth, or would they continue to reflect the "true fundamentals"?' This question goes to the nub of the debate between classical economics and believers in behavioural concepts such as reflexivity. True believers in reflexivity would even dispute the existence of such a thing as 'fundamentals', as understood in traditional approaches to market valuation. Soros emphasizes that market behaviour affects the 'fundamentals' through a whole host of different channels. In the 1990s mania these might be said to have included corporate profits being boosted as a result of investment gains made by companies investing in other ventures and also from pension fund gains, financial companies benefiting from the rise in the stock market, as well as companies benefiting from being able to substitute stock options for salaries, and earnings per share gains originating from acquisitions using highly priced paper. Some of these issues are discussed in the fourth and sixth chapters of this book, which look at investment approaches to valuation and asset allocation.

Taking the philosophical aspects of reflexivity versus fundamentalism even further, it might even be possible to question whether the measurement of the statistics themselves is independent of the climate of opinion regarding the variables to which they relate. In recent years probably the strongest consensus view held in the financial markets and amongst businesses has been the notion that inflation will inevitably remain extremely low, and that if there is any economic risk stemming from the overall pricing environment it is a risk posed by the possible threat of deflation. Against this background it has become conventional wisdom to suppose that the actual inflation numbers (which have in general remained consistently slightly higher than the prior expectations of financial markets) must be overstating true inflation because they have not adequately captured the ongoing improvements in the quality of goods such as computers. Governments have responded by making adjustments to the way in which inflation statistics are calculated, which have resulted in some reduction in measured inflation rates. Is this a case where the statistics have been adjusted to accord with expectations, rather than the other way round? This issue is touched on in Chapter 5, as part of a general discussion of the critical issue of whether the financial boom and bust of the last few years is genuinely deflationary (as most believe) or whether it will prove ultimately inflationary.

It is impossible to deny that reflexive behaviour does occur in financial markets and that there is interaction between the behaviour of markets and the behaviour of businesses. However, I would contend that the purely behavioural approach largely overlooks the role of money and credit in the business cycle, and as a result can never provide a complete explanation of the behaviour of financial markets. There is a tendency to assume that money and credit are endogenous to the mania (that is they are determined by the cycle) and that they are therefore merely another part of the 'feedback loop' that sustains the mania. In reality, this can only be true if the monetary authorities (the central bank) are permissive.

It is true that a mania will increase the demand for credit in the economy. As a stock market bubble develops, for instance, investors will be extrapolating the high returns from owning stocks into the future, which will mean that the demand for credit (for speculative purposes) will be stronger at any given level of interest rates than it was prior to the beginning of the bubble. If the central bank leaves interest rates unchanged, or raises them only slightly, as the stock market bubble gathers momentum then there will inevitably be greater credit extension. This will be associated with higher growth in the money supply, as the central bank remains accommodative. If the bubble persists then new business opportunities that depend on the existence of the bubble will emerge, further boosting the demand for credit through a greater number of channels.

Credit demand – and therefore money supply growth – will have a tendency to accelerate as long as the returns that seem to be available in the bubble environment compare favourably with the interest rate (when the necessary adjustments are made for risk and tax factors). This increased liquidity in the economy will of course add further fuel to the bubble. Generally, however, before the process becomes completely out of hand, the central bank takes action, implementing successive hikes in interest rates. There can be a variety of reasons why the central bank begins raising interest rates. It may recognize that an asset price bubble is developing and believe that it needs to take action to prick the bubble before there are possible damaging consequences for the economy and a later, much larger, crash. Or, it may focus on money and credit growth as one of the determinants of its policy (a money supply targeting policy). Or, and most commonly, the asset price bubble and the associated increase in credit and money growth may be beginning to be associated with more generalized inflationary pressures in the economy, to which the central bank is obliged to respond.

Whatever the reason for them, at some stage the increases in central bank interest rates and the associated squeeze on liquidity in the economy are enough to halt the rise in asset prices, and eventually reverse it. Once perceived returns from the assets that have been the object of speculation drop clearly relative to interest rates then the process that created the mania goes into reverse, in a manner well described by Kindleberger. As perceived returns are then falling sharply, a modest cut in interest rates by the central bank will not be enough to reverse what by then becomes a credit and monetary contraction. Only an aggressive reversal in policy by the central bank will forestall the process by which a market fall becomes a crash and then an outright financial panic and crisis, usually with deflationary consequences as in the US in the 1930s or Japan in the 1990s.

The point here is that although a reflexive tendency (that is feedback effects) is necessarily part of the mania (by definition it has to be, because a mania is by definition a behavioural phenomenon, irrational from the perspective of classical economics), a financial mania cannot be understood without reference to the policy of the central bank. The central bank is responsible for the liquidity that provides the fuel for the mania. If it acts passively to allow the mania to be associated with the creation of credit, then this will extend the mania but this process only occurs by dint of the central bank having made an implicit decision to act passively. The central bank is exogenous to the system (that is an outside influence upon the system) and the decisions it makes are decisive in determining the way in which the mania does or does not develop.

The position of the members of the central bank's interest rate-setting committee is completely different from that of all other participants in the financial markets or the economy. They are few in number but their decisions on interest rates and the provision of liquidity to the banking system and the economy are of far greater importance in determining the course of events than the decisions of other participants. This point seems to be overlooked in much writing on behavioural finance. Of course, the same thinking that is prevalent in the financial markets may influence the central bankers responsible for setting interest rates. In a mania they themselves may believe in the justifications for asset price inflation being put forward by the market participants. In December 1996 Federal Reserve Board chairman Alan Greenspan made his famous remark about Wall Street being infected with 'irrational exuberance'. But by 1999, as stock markets had continued on an accelerating path, Greenspan appeared to be convinced that the rise in market prices was in fact justified by a productivity miracle in the economy owing to the spread of the new technologies. In essence, the Fed had become part of the dynamics of the mania.

Nevertheless, the fact that central bankers themselves can become bound up in the same way of thinking as market participants and end up believing in the justifications for an asset price mania does not invalidate traditional monetary cycle analysis. If we wish to understand the medium- to long-term behaviour of the financial markets and the economy (that is the business cycle) it is the actions of the central bank that count, not the reasons for those actions. The actions of the central bank manifest in the rate of money and credit growth, which are determining influences over the course of the business cycle and the behaviour of the financial markets. This is discussed in the third chapter of this book.

Furthermore, central banks' actions in the modern world economy are constrained by the behaviour of inflation. Many central banks have explicit inflation targets and most of those that do not are still obliged to conduct policy with a view to keeping inflation low. It is the fact that US inflation remained low throughout the second half of the 1990s, even as the business cycle expansion became increasingly extended, that gave the Fed latitude to consider the possibility of a 'productivity miracle' and other aspects of the 'new era' thinking that typified the stock market mania. It is my contention in this book that the unprecedented length of the secular bull market in stocks from the beginning of the 1980s, and the unprecedented scale of the mania that was its conclusion, had structural consequences for the US and global economy such that the mania became a structural phenomenon as much as a cyclical one. It is interesting to consider whether this 'structural mania' could have had 'feedback effects' which themselves helped to suppress inflation. Most financial market participants and observers would probably dismiss this possibility out of hand, but in reality for the US economy in particular there are feedback channels from the stock market to inflation and inflation expectations that can be clearly identified. The issue of whether or not these are important is crucial to understanding what will be the final outcome of the fallout from the end of the secular bull market. These issues are discussed in Chapter 5, on 'Inflation or Deflation', and in the concluding chapter of this book.

Part of the structural picture is undoubtedly the way in which the industry of investment itself developed during the secular bull market. A complete analysis of this, encompassing banking and investment banking, would require another, large, book but a small part of the picture – that concerning the fund management industry – is touched upon in Chapter 6.

My own personal experience of asset management began in 1981 when I joined the asset management firm GT Management. In its heyday of rapid growth GT Management grew its personnel largely by hiring talented people when the opportunity presented itself and finding a place for them in an evolving structure. Investment featured a disciplined analysis of relevant economic developments and of individual companies but asset allocation decisions were, in the end, judgemental and not overly influenced by the composition of indices. Today parts of the hedge fund industry and investment boutiques still operate in a similar manner, but the mainstream fund management companies do not. The influence, in particular, of the pension fund consultancy industry has driven the fund managers progressively to more and more quantitative approaches, where the emphasis is on structure and process.

In my most recent jobs I had cause to be struck by the degree to which the asset management industry has changed over the past twenty or so years. In the most recent company I worked for, an investment department was put together following a merger. The management created the new department from the two old operations by first deciding on an optimal structure – expressed by a complex of 'organograms' – and then identifying the people who could be slotted into the various boxes in the structure. Inevitably there were plenty of boxes for process-oriented areas such as 'risk control' that would not have existed twenty years earlier. In some cases there were boxes but no people to fill them and in other cases talented people with no boxes.

The modern emphasis on structure and process in institutional investment is understandable because people cannot be relied upon to stay in the same jobs for long. Pension funds and their consultants therefore naturally feel more comfortable with the notion that it is the structure of the team that is managing their money and the processes that the team is using that are important, rather than the individuals that comprise the team. In the

1980s and 1990s pension fund consultants began to put a great deal of emphasis on how research, whether on economic and market developments or on sectors or companies, translated into the actual allocation of assets in the pension fund portfolio and the measurement and control of the risks involved. This has driven the industry to greater and greater use of quantitative methods and processes to estimate expected returns from different asset classes and to measure the risk inherent in different asset allocations.

The problem with the emphasis on structure and process is that financial market behaviour is not amenable to being described by comparatively rigid statistical models. This is one of the conclusions that can correctly be drawn from the ideas of behavioural finance. But the processes that were increasingly employed by an ever-larger part of the industry during the 1990s – with their implicit emphasis on price and earnings momentum, earnings growth expectations and bond yield-earnings yield ratios in particular – surely played their part in building and extending the financial market mania in the accommodative monetary environment that central banks permitted. A lesson that ought to be learned from the collapse of the giant growth stock bubble is that these methods do not work, but, at the time of writing in late 2002, there is little evidence that the key lessons have been fully understood.

Inevitably in parts of this book – particularly in Chapter 2 – I will appear critical of those who encouraged investors into taking an active part in the 1990s stock market mania with their convincing-sounding pseudo-economics and quack analysis. To some, this might look a little like being wise after the event. After all, it is easy to be critical with the benefit of hindsight. With this in mind, in the final chapter of this book I have tried to look into the future myself, drawing the conclusions from what I believe is the sound economic and financial analysis presented here.

Because the asset price bubble of the 1990s encompassed more than merely the stock market – at the time of writing government bonds remain very seriously over-priced on any assessment of long-term realistic value – and because of the structural nature of the bubble, its full unwinding will be a very long process. This does not necessarily mean that global stock markets will be in a downward trend for years to come. However, it is likely to mean that what worked for investors for most of the 1990s will not work over the next decade, both in terms of investment approaches and specific areas of investment. The possible implications for the global economy and the financial markets are the subject of the concluding chapter.

CHAPTER 2

The Greatest Financial Bubble of All Time

'The fate of the world economy is now totally dependent on the growth of the US economy, which is dependent on the stock market, whose growth is dependent on about 50 stocks, half of which have never reported any earnings.'

(Paul Volcker, 14 May 1999)

Internet Mania

In each of the five years from 1995 to 1999 the Standard and Poor's Composite Index of the US stock market (S&P 500) gave investors an annual total return (including dividends) in excess of 20 per cent. Previously in history this had never happened for even three consecutive years. Furthermore these five years were the culmination of a 20-year period during which the S&P 500 returned investors an unprecedented 17.9 per cent annualized. In comparison, in the 55 years up to 1980 US stocks had returned a much more modest 9.4 per cent on an annual total return basis.

This secular bull market in US stocks is usually understood to have begun on 12 August 1982, in the midst of the 1981–82 recession, although its origin could be dated back as far as 1978. Figure 2.1, which is charted in logarithmic terms so that a steady rise in the index line represents a constant percentage rate of appreciation, shows a clear acceleration in the rate of ascent of the market from 1995.

Towards the end of this period the market's performance was increasingly concentrated in the stocks of large companies and of growth companies (that is companies that had been delivering strong growth in earnings per share and were expected to continue to do so), particularly in the 'hot' areas of technology, media and telecommunications (TMT). The NASDAQ Composite index of over-the-counter stocks, which has a heavy representation in technology shares, experienced a further acceleration to an even steeper rate of ascent from late 1998. The NASDAQ only reached the level of 2,000 for the first time during 1998 but it had crossed 5,000 by the time it recorded its closing high of 5,048 on 10 March 2000.

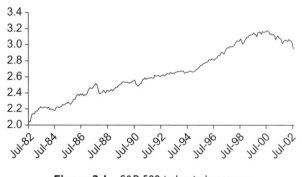

Figure 2.1   S&P 500 index in log terms

Source: Thomson Financial Datastream

These years, 1998–2000, were the years of internet euphoria. The internet as a stock market phenomenon began with the initial public offering (IPO) of Netscape in August 1995. By 1998 the internet share bubble had become a mania the like of which has never been seen before and almost certainly never will be again. Companies such as Amazon.com and Yahoo! were given values measured in tens of billions of dollars. Yahoo! was valued at as much as US$139 billion at its peak. By March 1999 AOL, with a stock market capitalization of US$140 billion, was worth more than Walt Disney, Viacom and CBS combined, and well over twice as much as General Motors (about US$60 billion at that time).

In many ways more staggering than the market capitalizations of these 'household name' internet companies were the values that the market was giving to brand new companies that, to the seasoned eye, were quite obviously worthless. Internet grocery company Webvan reached a peak market capitalization of over US$8 billion shortly after its stock market debut in November 1999. The *Wall Street Journal* noted that this was close to half the market value of Safeway, even though the *annual* sales revenues of Webvan would have been for Safeway only a good afternoon's. Webvan eventually closed its doors in July 2001, having consumed about US$1 billion of investors' money without ever making a profit. E*Toys was another, similar, story. This company had sales of only about US$20 million in the first half of 1999 but by late 1999 investors were valuing it as worth far more than Toys R Us, giving it a market capitalization of US$5.4 *billion* (compared with Toys R Us's market capitalization of US$3.7 billion on sales of US$4.3 billion). E*Toys eventually went out of business in March 2001.

Webvan at least invested in a huge warehousing and distribution network with the aim of creating a sustainable business, even if this aim ultimately proved unachievable. Most internet companies spent the cash received through stock financings – 'cash burn' as it was known in the jargon – on advertising. The idea at the time was that the survivors in a very competitive market would be the companies that had built brand recognition, and that massive advertising expenditure was therefore a must. In the period leading up to Christmas 1999 – a 'make or break' time for many of the consumer internet companies that had by then started up – advertising spend by the US internet industry was estimated to have exploded to an annualized rate of US$7.5 billion, a huge amount for what were completely new companies.

This was the era of 'day trading' and heavy participation in the stock market by individual investors. Money poured into mutual funds such as the Munder 'NetNet fund', a mutual fund traded over the internet that invested in stocks of internet companies. Stories abounded of people quitting good jobs to spend all day trading stocks at specialized day trading centres. In early 1999 it was estimated that in excess of US$5 billion each day was being traded in the stock market by full-time day-traders executing up to 30–40 trades a day each. Added to this was the trading of over seven million holders of online retail brokerage accounts, nearly a quarter of a million of which were making multiple trades per day. On very active internet chat rooms or bulletin boards, such as trading-places.net or Motley Fool, tipsters ramped up individual stocks by creating or passing on rumours. Online 'hot-stock alert services', such as Tokyo Joe's, were able to move the prices of stocks sharply, as legions of followers responded to their recommendations. The *Wall Street Journal* carried articles about taxi drivers trading internet stocks from their cabs. And, of course, all this business was marvellous for the online brokerage companies themselves. By the Spring of 1999, there were 92 of them, according to the *Financial Times*, and the largest, Charles Schwab, had a stock market capitalization 50 per cent larger than that of Merrill Lynch.

The internet appeared to be producing countless new millionaires, and many billionaires. Company founders and large shareholders such as Jay Walker of Priceline.com, Mark Cuban of Broadcast.com and Naveen Jain of InfoSpace.com measured their wealth – on paper, at least – in the billions. According to a *Financial Times* article of 10 December 1999 even the students who had had part-time and holiday jobs at Akamai Technologies were millionaires from the stock options they had been granted. Akamai, a company in the business of making web sites faster and more reliable, was formed only in 1998 and launched on the stock market in October 1999. Its closing share price on its first day of trading gave it a market value in excess of US$13 *billion* even though its annual *sales* were running at under US$2 *million*. At the peak of the market investors were valuing it at an enormous US$22 billion.

Venture capital funds were overflowing with money destined for would-be internet companies. The US National Venture Capital Association estimated that venture capital investment well over doubled in 1999, to

US$48.3 billion, with internet companies accounting for two-thirds of this money. The idea was to finance start-ups until they could be brought to the stock market, preferably as quickly as possible. In 1999 rarely a week went past without a considerable number of internet IPOs. The general pattern was that the offer price would be increased at least once before the stock market launch and that the stock would close at a massive first-day premium in the wake of huge speculation. But buyers at this price often found themselves in losses fairly quickly. TheGlobe.com set a then-record on its IPO of 12 November 1998 when its stock closed at a 606 per cent premium to its offer price. But, having reached a peak capitalization of US$769 million in April 1999, TheGlobe.com had fallen to under US$5 million by the end of 2000.

For many companies coming later to the market the period during which the average investor could make money was even briefer. This was particularly the case for the companies catering for the consumer market (B2C). Community web site iVillage reached a peak capitalization of over US$2.6 billion, but this was within days of its launch on the stock market in April 1999. Towards the end of 2000 its market value had crashed to under US$20 million. Relative latecomers to the internet boom such as Pets.com or Garden.com saw their share prices falling away straight from their IPOs. Pets.com initially came to the stock market in February 2000 but, after the briefest moment of stock market glory, by November 2000 it had been closed down.

A stock market flotation was deemed essential for an internet company because these companies were loss-making and they needed finance, and they also needed a 'currency' for acquisitions. During the frenzy internet companies were able to boost market value simply by splitting their stock or merging with other loss-making companies, seemingly magically creating huge additional stock market wealth. On 12 October 1999 the *Financial Times* reported that Phone.com was buying a Dublin-based information technology company, Apion, in an all-stock deal. Phone.com's share price had already risen 12-fold since debuting on the stock market four months earlier, but the news of its acquisition added another 12 per cent to its market value, defying the norm that shares in an acquiring company generally fall on the announcement of an acquisition.

Executives left good jobs to join internet start-ups. Established companies tried to refashion themselves as internet stocks. Alternatively, they spun off online subsidiaries as separate entities or issued 'tracking stocks' tied to their online operations, hugely boosting total market value in the process. Professional firms – lawyers, consultants, public relations companies – were happy to take equity stakes in internet companies in lieu of fees for services they provided.

Internet mania continued until the NASDAQ peaked in March 2000, although by then enthusiasm had shifted from the consumer companies (B2C) to the internet companies whose customers were businesses rather than consumers (B2B), including companies that were creating trading platforms for all manner of business supplies and commodities. At the peak of the market the favourites were companies such as B2B company Commerce One, corporate internet services provider PSINet, which reached a peak market value of US$8.2 billion on 6 March 2000, and internet 'incubator' CMGI, which also peaked in early 2000 at around US$35 billion. CMGI rose 10-fold in 1999. On the NASDAQ market there were 37 stocks that showed gains of 1,000 per cent or more for that year.

During the mania hardly any internet companies were actually making profits. By the peak there were plenty of companies being accorded huge values by investors that had virtually no revenues. Professional investor John Dorfman, in an article carried by *Bloomberg News* on 17 February 2000, worked out that 28 of the 408 US companies with a stock market value of over US$6 billion not only had little earnings, they had very little in the way of revenue. Amongst other companies, he singled out Intertrust Technologies, a Californian maker of e-commerce software. With commendable honesty the company's report for the Securities and Exchange Commission carried the following statements, according to Dorfman: 'Our licensees have not yet used our technology in the commercial distribution of their products and we have not earned any transaction fees under this business model. If our technology is commercially released, the volume of products and services distributed using our technology may be too small to support or grow our business', and: 'We have a history of losses, and we expect our operating expenses and losses to increase significantly.' Yet investors were valuing Intertrust at a staggering US$7.6 billion.

In the eyes of some, profits – and perhaps even revenues – were a liability because they provided an old-fashioned basis for valuing a company. For believers, the internet was all about potential, not profits in the here and now. With no price-to-earnings ratios there was no limit to the values the market could ascribe to these companies. Analysts invented new methods of valuing them, which towards the end of the bubble employed some fairly heavyweight mathematical concepts. At the peak of the market, in the spring of 2000, interested investors could have spent US$3,000 or thereabouts to attend conferences such as one in London organized by Euromoney Training on 'Valuing Hi-Tech Companies'. This course promised to teach delegates how to 'value internet stocks using price/sales and value per customer ratios' and how to 'account for the gaps between conventional and observed valuations (option value of companies, intangible assets, first mover advantage)' with 'reference to leading internet companies'. This particular two-day course contained sessions discussing 'The limitations of ratio-driven valuations', 'The option character of high technology plays' and sessions such as 'Evaluating strategy in the internet space'. In the publicity material delegates were promised that they would 'develop [their] knowledge of internet valuation terminology and techniques' and 'apply the most versatile and flexible valuation techniques to internet firms'.

A similar conference organized by ICM Conferences over 17–18 April 2000, also in London, promised attendees that amongst the 'valuable benefits' they would take from the event would be the ability to 'identify the opportunities in each internet sector: connection, community, content, commerce' and to 'understand the business models of tomorrow and how they will affect company valuations today'. Under the session on valuation methodology, entitled 'Internet companies are like options – winners will be able to exercise them and capture the value', the first discussion point was listed in the programme as 'Traditional valuation methods do not work when looking at valuing internet stocks'.

The publicity material for the Euromoney course noted that the value of US internet stocks alone was above US$2 trillion at the time, 'making these stocks nearly as valuable as the entire UK market'. Of course, it could be added that the UK market itself was grossly inflated by excessively valued technology and telecommunications shares. More pertinent perhaps was the fact that by the March peak a widely followed index of internet stocks had risen almost eight-fold in only 18 months. The NASDAQ Composite as a whole had more than tripled and was trading on over 200 times the earnings per share of the component companies. The internet companies, of course, were not making any profits at all. In their book *The Internet Bubble*, published in November 1999, Anthony B. Perkins and Michael C. Perkins had calculated that, even on optimistic assumptions for profit margins and long-term sustainable price earnings ratios, the companies in the US e-commerce sector would still need to grow revenues by nearly 90 per cent annually for the following five years to justify valuations as at June 1999.[4] The final peak valuations for the internet sector as a whole were much higher still than these levels.

Internet mania was far from purely a US phenomenon. By its peak it had spread around the world, leaving little of the globe untouched. A flavour can be gleaned from the 'Companies and Markets' section of the UK edition of the *Financial Times* of 25 February 2000 – a date close to the climax of the internet frenzy. On that day this section of this most respected of business newspapers carried a staggering 22 internet-related company stories. These included 'United News may float its web assets', 'Reed may win applause if internet ambitions are realised', 'Avis to launch used-car web site', 'EDP to relaunch as Fastfreenet.com', 'ABN Amro to invest €1.8

billion in e-commerce', 'Carrefour plans internet expansion' and 'Two Swedish internet groups agree to merge', amongst many others.

In many ways, at its end the mania outside the US was even more extreme than the US version, and some of the valuations achieved by companies in the stock market even more unbelievable. In Spain, Terra Networks, a spin-off from telecommunications operator Telefonica, soared to a market capitalization of €25 billion, making it the fourth biggest company in Spain despite having no profits. Investors in Italian internet group Tiscali saw its share price rise 20-fold in its first four months as a public company, overtaking the market value of Fiat in the process. A table from the UK edition of the *Financial Times* of 27 March 2000, listing pending European equity issues, contained no less than 10 internet companies about to come to the market for equity finance. In the UK stocks such as Freeserve and smaller internet stocks such as QXL.com and internet 'incubator' NewMedia Spark, echoed the US experience, while the co-founders of Lastminute.Com, the photogenic Brent Hoberman and Martha Lane Fox, were the entrepreneurial heroes of the day and rarely out of newspapers and magazines.

In Asia the exponential rise of internet stock Softbank allowed investors in Japan some respite from their multi-year bear market. In Hong Kong Pacific Century Cyberworks was able to buy Hong Kong's dominant telecommunications company Cable & Wireless HKT despite being only 10 months old and having no profits and minimal revenues. Police were called in to control the crowds queuing to apply for the IPO of Tom.com, over-subscribed by 669 times. This internet company had no profits, no revenues to speak of, and reportedly a web site that, at the time of flotation, was 'under construction'.

An unusual feature of internet mania was that it co-existed with fairly widespread scepticism. There was a mini-publishing industry in books predicting an imminent crash before it even happened, which may be unique in the history of financial bubbles. The aforementioned book *The Internet Bubble* was particularly unusual in that the authors came from within the internet industry. The book *Irrational Exuberance* by Yale University academic Professor Robert Shiller was also published at the peak of the market.[5] Professor Shiller was concerned with the US stock market as a whole, but he identified the internet phenomenon as a key factor behind the stock market mania. Influential academic economist Paul Krugman was another sceptic. In an interview in June 1999, Krugman was quoted as saying, 'If you are looking for the world's biggest risk, I would probably put it in my home country – if you are looking for a bubble that can burst, it's back in the US.'

Financial journalists and columnists, particularly those with the UK papers such as the *Financial Times* and *The Economist*, were consistently sceptical about internet stock valuations and very negative about the way the US stock market as a whole was developing through 1999, correctly identifying it as a bubble that would ultimately burst. So much so that one reader, an irritated and bullish fund management executive from the US, felt moved to write to a UK newspaper in November 1999:

> 'I want to say how impressed I continue to be with the inability of your journalists to predict correctly the demise of the US bull market. We have seen many, many articles on this subject over the past decade. This pessimistic attitude continues to permeate the City of London. No wonder I read that investment managers are being sued for their performance ... this extraordinary flow of money into new technologies, new ideas and new jobs seems to me a more attractive place than bidding up Greater London real estate prices once again.'

Also, it is only fair to mention that some amongst the now much-maligned investment banking community were highly sceptical, in fact overtly negative, on the internet stocks and the US market. Investment bank HSBC published a 52-page piece of research in July 1999, written by their economists and entitled 'The US bubble and how it will burst'. And Morgan Stanley Dean Witter, although probably destined to be remembered for their bullish star internet analyst, 'Net Queen' Mary Meeker, produced countless negative market research pieces throughout 1999 and early 2000 written by their veteran strategists Barton Biggs and Byron Wien and economist Stephen Roach. Biggs, in particular, recognized internet mania for what it was throughout.

In fact it is commonplace now for investment professionals and information technology industry executives to claim that they knew all along that the internet stock market phenomenon was a huge mania, destined to end very badly, but that they had no option at the time but to be involved. This may have been true for some, or even many, but not for all. Otherwise, how can we explain Goldman Sachs's analysts telling investors, 'Webvan has reengineered the back-end fulfilment system to create a scalable solution to the last-mile problem of e-commerce.' Or Dresdner Kleinwort Benson's Europe team in London writing, on 9 March 2000 – the day before the market top – that 'Individuals may be stupid, but the market as a whole is quite canny. The visions for the future have probably been discounted to a greater extent than the individual can imagine, but it is unlikely that they are fully reflected in prices. TMT will remain the key sectors for the market in the period ahead.' Or indeed the chief executive of Compaq Computer, Eckard Pfeiffer, who was reported as saying, 'The internet is a revolution that is happening and is changing the world, so you cannot measure what is happening here with the metrics of what we are used to.'

Research that promoted the internet and technology stock market boom was also put out by other major securities houses, including Merrill Lynch. Then Chief Economist Bruce Steinberg produced a research piece in October 1999 entitled 'The US Economy is No Bubble'. A section of this note carried the title 'The Equity Market is Not Overvalued'. Even after the enormous volatility that accompanied the March 2000 top of the NASDAQ and the steepness of the initial decline that followed, a very large part – probably the majority – of the industry remained bullish. Comments to the press such as this from the chief executive of Aberdeen Asset Management, a UK fund management company, were typical in the spring of 2000: 'People are still buying the [technology] funds, even in the dips. Maybe there's a more sophisticated investor out there' (*Financial Times,* 3 May 2000). Goldman Sachs's super-bull, Abby Joseph Cohen, should not go unmentioned either. While not specifically an internet stock enthusiast, she more than anyone was the spokesperson for the whole bull market of the 1990s, encouraging investors with her persistently positive stance on the US stock market and economy. Exactly a year into the bear market, in March 2001, she was still bullish, telling a conference of executives and financial analysts, 'Today the S&P 500, while it was overvalued a year ago, is now undervalued ... we are in the midst of the most structurally sound economy that the United States has ever seen and most likely the most structurally sound economy the world has ever seen ... we have now returned to an overweight in tech and telecoms.' At that time she was predicting the Dow Jones Industrial Average at 13,000 by the end of 2001.

In the late stages of the bull market, the investment world was split between sceptics and believers in a 'new era'. The problem was that by its peak the mania had gone on for so long – out-lasting all previous similar episodes – that sceptics had been sceptical for too long and, in many cases, had lost a great deal of money betting against the market. The success, and the resources, were with the believers. The way the investment industry works, asset management companies are not able to defy such a persistent trend in the market indefinitely. This is discussed in more depth later in this book, in Chapter 6, but a significant element of the problem can be summarized in part with a quote from a piece on Groupthink, written in 1999 by Morgan Stanley's Biggs: 'On an investment committee, it is almost better to be wrong with the group than to express a contrary view, even if it is right, because if by any chance you are both wrong and a dissident, you are finished as a functioning member of the committee or firm.'[6] In an investment organization there is a fundamental inconsistency between the need to progress in the organization – which requires being an 'insider' – and taking a contrary view – which by definition means being an 'outsider'.

In the last months of the mania there were countless examples of professional investors 'throwing in the towel' and capitulating to the accelerating trend of the technology stocks, bringing more money into these stocks in the process. Legendary hedge fund manager Julian Robertson closed down his Tiger Management funds in March 2000, after assets had shrunk from US$22 billion to US$6 billion in less than two years as a result of poor performance and investors withdrawing funds. Robertson's funds had largely ignored internet and other technology stocks, believing them to be grossly overvalued. The managers of George Soros's Quantum and Quota funds were sucked in to the high-tech stocks at a late stage, leaving those funds taking heavy losses when these stocks crashed in March and April 2000, and forcing Soros to reorganize and scale down his operation. In the UK, the defining moment of the time was perhaps the resignation of Tony Dye as the head of investment at value investment fund management house Phillips & Drew. Under Dye's leadership Phillips & Drew had been famous in the UK investment world for shunning the technology stocks in favour of more reasonably valued shares, with the result that the performance of the pension funds they managed had inevitably been poor. In January 2000 Phillips & Drew announced that they were going to rethink their investment strategy to find ways to accommodate technology in their portfolios. As a result Dye was forced to step down, just before the final peak of the technology bubble and the big switch to out-performance by value stocks in the stock market.

The 'New Economy'

By the end of the 1990s the majority of active fund managers and fund management houses had a growth investment style (that is they preferred to invest in stocks that had high earnings growth and that were expected to continue to enjoy strong earnings growth) rather than employing a value-based approach (that is buying stocks that appear cheap on various criteria). Growth had not always meant high technology. In the early 1990s pharmaceuticals were a favoured sector of the global stock market and in the mid-1990s consumer brands, such as Coca Cola and Gillette, were fashionable. However, by the end of the 1990s growth and technology had become virtually synonymous in the eyes of many growth fund managers. As one stockbroker put it colourfully – and rather crudely – at the time, 'Growth fund managers are attracted to technology like flies to shit.' Perhaps, to be fair, we should also include the other parts of the 'TMT' concept – media and telecoms – along with technology.

In truth many professional growth investors were dubious about the valuations accorded to the internet stocks, which they recognized as ludicrously overvalued. However, they all believed that the internet, computer networking in general, and the advances taking place in telecommunications were bringing about a 'new economy' that obeyed different rules from those that were familiar to conventional economists. In this 'new paradigm' the opportunities for growth, particularly in the information technology industry, were considered to be almost limitless. As far as the stock market was concerned, historic valuation norms were therefore thought to be irrelevant for the technology stocks that were poised to benefit from this 'new economy', companies such as networking equipment group Cisco Systems or fibre-optic component maker JDS Uniphase.

Central bankers and governments did not exactly discourage these beliefs. At a US Federal Reserve meeting, Federal Reserve Bank of New York President William McDonough was reported as saying, in September 1999, 'If you look at the individual stocks ... it is very difficult not to reach the conclusion that individual stocks are behaving very rationally.' He pointed to technology as the main driver of the long-running US expansion. In March 2000, at the time of the market peak, McDonough was again quoted: 'I am quite sure we don't have a bubble economy in the United States.' Dallas Federal Reserve Bank President Robert McTeer was known as the Fed governor most consistently optimistic on the implications of the 'new economy'. In an interview in October 1999, he was asked to respond to the views being given in *The Economist* news magazine, which perceived the 'new economy' as merely a giant bubble that was bound to burst. 'To say that they are right means that you know more than all the people who are buying stocks. More than the market ... ' was one of his comments. Fed Governor Laurence Meyer had been a 'new economy' sceptic, but by the autumn of 1999 he had largely been converted. In a speech in October 1999 he said, 'It is true that the rise in equity prices – averaging 25 per cent to 30 per cent a year over the last four years – is unprecedented and that current values challenge previous valuation standards.' But he went on to suggest that the structural changes in the economy might provide a justification: 'Such structural changes could, in principle, justify at least a substantial portion of the rise in equity prices.'

Outside the US, central bankers and government spokespeople also gave their, at least qualified, support to the US equity market and economy. The normally cautious Eddie George, the governor of the Bank of England, reported on a meeting of central bankers in December 1999 as follows:

'On the whole, the discussion suggested that the particular strengths of high-technology stocks in equity markets provided a better underpinning of equity values than perhaps had been appreciated ... That explains a good deal of the strength of equity markets so that if anything, perhaps that meant that the strength of equities could be better sustained and certainly it has been sustained.'

In Spain, Economy Minister Rodrigo Rato exhorted the benefits of the stock market in February 2000: 'The stock market is one of the new opportunities where for a normal family to place their savings ... it makes no difference the time scale that you choose, five, ten or twenty years, everyone wins.' The OECD (Organisation for Economic Co-operation and Development) had also grown to love the 'new economy' by the spring of 2000. In their report on the US, they stated, 'The US economy seems to have shifted to a higher potential growth path, having recovered a significant amount of the dynamism lost in the 1970s and 1980s ... Such a durable increase in output is linked to a significant economic transformation.'

On the other side of the ledger, the IMF, the US National Association for Business Economics and the US Securities and Exchange Commission all expressed concern about the risk of a stock market crash and the impact it would have on investors and the economy. For the central bankers, the governor of the Norwegian central bank deserves an honourable mention, for saying in his annual speech, in February 2000, 'The so-called new economy may be a bubble. The very expression "new economy" was first mentioned ahead of what was the great stock market crash of 1929.'

For fund managers in 1999 and 2000 all of these views were as nothing compared with the views and sayings of one particular person – Alan Greenspan, the US Federal Reserve chairman, known as the 'Maestro'. To bullish fund managers, for an economist or other commentator to claim he knew better than the market was bad enough, but for him to claim to know better than Alan Greenspan verged on sacrilege. Greenspan, after all, as head of the Fed since 1987 was the man who had guided the US economy through its longest expansion in modern history, keeping inflation down while presiding over a booming economy and the largest increase in wealth ever seen in such a comparatively short period. In December 1996, Greenspan had famously questioned whether Wall Street was displaying 'irrational exuberance': 'How do we know when irrational exuberance has unduly escalated asset values ... and how do we factor that assessment into monetary policy?' By 1999 Greenspan had largely come to believe in the 'new economy' and its supposed benefits for productivity, inflation and stock prices. In his semi-annual Humphrey-Hawkins economic report to Congress in February 2000 Greenspan told the Senate Banking Committee, 'The best I can say to you is that it is certainly true that we have a new economy. It is different. It is behaving differently and it requires a different type of monetary policy to maintain its stability and growth than we had in the past.' In answer to a question, he said, 'the issue of stock prices and equity values generally going up as a consequence of accelerating productivity is a perfectly understandable and appropriate thing to happen. That is, the real value of assets has indeed increased.'

The evidence for a 'new economy' was an apparent shift upwards, from the mid-1990s, in the rate of growth the US economy could achieve without triggering inflation. Productivity growth seemed to have moved to a higher trend rate, labour productivity growth averaging somewhat over 2 per cent annually from 1995–99, as opposed to little more than 1 per cent over the previous 25 years. Increasingly, in the late 1990s, traditional economists who had persistently been warning that inflation was bound to begin to rise given the extended period of high economic growth, and given the accompanying steep fall in the unemployment rate, looked to all the world to have been 'crying wolf'. Estimates of the long-run achievable growth rate of the US economy began to rise, with the growing band of believers in a 'new paradigm' arguing that the US economy could well be capable of growing at least 4 per cent annually on a sustained basis, perhaps much more, compared with the roughly 2.5 per cent that had been thought in the past to be the growth 'limit'.

The theory for a 'new economy' rested on a number of interconnected ideas, the buzzwords for which were 'globalization', 'network effects' and 'scalability'. The idea was that the world economy had become increasingly a 'weightless economy'. Whereas 50 years earlier much of the industrialized countries' output was physical output such as cars and other consumer goods and machinery, now the bulk of GDP comprised services of various types. Information had become much more important than physical commodities such as steel or copper. Furthermore, the world was becoming one big 'globalized' economy rather than a large number of separate, independent, economies. Countries' economies were interdependent and companies were selling into a competitive world market.

Computers had been around for a long time but, the story went, businesses had only learned how to maximize the potential of computers for increased efficiency with the development of computer networks in the 1990s. Then came the advances in telecommunications, mobile telephony, and, most importantly, the internet. The internet was subject to the economics of networks – 'Metcalfe's Law' – which states that the value of the network is related to the square of its users. If only two people in the world own a telephone then a telephone only has limited use, but as increasingly more people own a telephone then the usefulness of the telephone increases exponentially for its users. In the case of the internet, the development of 'B2B' marketplaces where companies could easily identify the cheapest sources of supply in the world and buy the cheapest materials and components, and 'B2C' possibilities for companies to sell directly over the internet, promised huge increases in efficiency, lower costs of production and 'cutting out the middle man' to the advantage of consumers.

The 'new economy' adherents thought that supply in the economy could be increased almost without limit. There might be no 'speed limit' at all to the economy's possible growth rate. In a world where competition would be so complete – 'perfect competition', in the economists' parlance, on a global scale – then inflation, supposedly, could not occur. No businesses would have the ability to raise prices – 'pricing power' – because they would lose their market straight away. With no possibility of inflation, there could be no recessions, because traditionally the only reason for recessions had been that inflation had tended to get out of hand once strong economic growth had been sustained for too long.

These characteristics of the 'new economy' were thought to be reinforced by 'scalability'. This is the idea that within the knowledge and information-based economy the cost of producing new units of output is negligible after the initial investment has been made. For instance, the producer of a research report can send out more copies on his e-mail at no real cost. So the unit cost of production falls dramatically the more copies of the report that can be sold. Traditional economics assumed the law of diminishing returns. Producing more output tended to result in rising marginal costs – and there-fore the price of the product – at some level of output, because ultimately productivity would tend to drop as output increased. In the 'new economy', supposedly, there were increasing returns to scale.

The 'new economy' case can be summarized with a quote taken from an article written by economist and television commentator Lawrence Kudlow, written for the *Wall Street Journal* in August 1999, 'Why all the good news? Because the internet is more important than the Fed. Easily accessible, low-cost information and increased competition, the hallmarks of internet eco-nomics, will contribute substantially more growth with significantly lower prices ... Think of it as deflationary growth, a classic consequence of long-wave technology cycles' ('What's More Important than the Fed', the *Wall Street Journal Europe*, 30 August 1999).

This was the vision that investors, both professional and amateur, were buying into in 1999 and early 2000. During this period it was barely possible to watch US financial television channel CNBC without seeing a fund manag-er extolling the virtues of Cisco and JDS Uniphase, which appeared to be on every fund manager's list of favourite stocks. A typical comment was the fol-lowing, from the chief investment strategist at Kemper Funds in January 2000: 'It's a new world order. We see people discard all the right companies with the right people with the right vision because their stock price is too high. That's

the worst mistake an investor can make. The people who have missed the bull
market are the people who are on the sidelines trying to figure out how to value
these things as opposed to getting into the market.' Reportedly, this investment
strategist's advice was that investors should own Cisco Systems Inc., Motorola
Inc. and Intel Corp. at any price and not fret about valuations.

By the end of 1999 Cisco's stock market capitalization was US$366
billion and investors in the company had enjoyed a total return of 2,645 per
cent over the prior five years. It was to go higher, surpassing US$400 bil-
lion in market capitalization at the beginning of February 2000 and then
half a trillion dollars by the market peak in March, making it the largest
company in the world by market value. Three market favourite high-tech
companies – Cisco, Microsoft and Oracle – were together worth over
US$1.3 trillion, comparable in size to the annual GDP of the UK economy.
The US information technology sector as a whole had a stock market value
of around US$3 trillion, greater than the entire UK equity market and about
nine times the size of the whole global mining industry. The 15 biggest
US technology stocks were worth more than the whole US stock market
a decade earlier.

In March 2000 Cisco was estimated to be trading on a price–earnings
ratio of around 200 times its 1999 profits and 32 times its revenues.
Estimates suggested that the company would need to grow revenues by
50 per cent annually for many years to come to justify that valuation. Yet
many investors thought that this was possible. Cisco, like many high-tech
companies, had very limited debt because with such high-priced equity it
was comfortably able to do any necessary financing through equity issuance.
It was therefore thought to be immune from interest rates, which had been
rising since mid-1999. The projections for the explosive growth of the internet and corporate computer networks, for which Cisco is a dominant sup-
plier of equipment, seemed to mean that Cisco's exceptionally rapid growth
was assured, regardless of the fate of the pure internet stocks. It was telling
that even after the collapse of the internet stocks began, in March and April
2000, the share price of Cisco held up remarkably well for several months.
Investors kept the faith, rotating out of the very speculative internet shares
into what were perceived to be 'blue-chips' such as Cisco.

What investors failed to see were the myriad ways in which Cisco and
the other large-capitalization high technology stocks had been benefiting
from the mania aspects of the internet boom as opposed to the genuine
growth that was undeniably there. Some of these were very direct. The large
high-tech companies were investing in and profiting from investments in
other high-tech companies and start-ups. Intel's investment portfolio was
reported to be worth US$8.2 billion alone at the end of 1999, compared
with only US$500 million two years earlier. They were also benefiting from

the huge equipment demands that the frenzy of technology investment by start-up internet companies, telecoms companies and 'old economy' companies, frightened of 'missing the boat', were generating. Cisco and other high-tech companies had been financing, to some extent, customers to buy its equipment. Once the downdraught in the market and in investment spending had taken hold, sales of its equipment by these and other information technology companies that had gone bankrupt helped to undermine the markets for its products, proving that a chunk of its sales during the boom were a function of the hype rather than the long-term growth prospects of the technology industry.

The large technology companies were also benefiting at least as much as their smaller brethren from the appreciation of their own stock prices and of the stock market as a whole. Employees could be compensated handsomely with stock options rather than 'real money', saving on salary costs. Other companies could be purchased with highly priced paper, allowing the acquirer effectively to buy earnings growth to satisfy the stock market. Cisco itself was enormously acquisitive, buying 70 companies at a rate of almost two a month over 1999–2000. Many of the companies purchased did not have profits but it was able to account for them aggressively to the benefit of its bottom line. These, and other, issues are discussed in more depth later in this book, in Chapter 6.

The communications infrastructure was as necessary to the 'new economy' as computers. Another US company in this area that out-performed even Cisco during the TMT mania was fibre-optic component maker JDS Uniphase. JDS's customers were telecom equipment makers such as Lucent Technologies and Nortel Networks. When telecoms spending collapsed in 2001, JDS had to take enormous write-downs reflecting the fact that acquisitions it had made during the boom were worth much less than had been

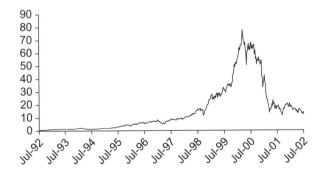

Figure 2.2 Cisco Systems share price

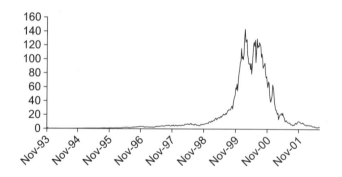

Figure 2.3 JDS Uniphase share price

believed, and also losses on its investments. By 2002 JDS Uniphase's share price had given back all that it had gained during the mania, as Figure 2.3 clearly shows.

In the telecommunications industry the crash of 2001–02 was in many ways more spectacular than the crash in the information technology industry, with the collapse in the share prices of very widely held shares such as Lucent and the bankruptcy of former high-fliers Global Crossing and WorldCom. WorldCom had been valued at roughly US$300 billion at its peak. In the UK Marconi, the once great company formerly known as GEC, was left virtually destroyed by a string of acquisitions of US telecoms equipment companies.

By the spring of 2000, at the peak of TMT mania, the scale of activity in the industry globally had been huge. In Europe six of the ten largest companies by market capitalization were telecoms companies, and mobile telephone companies were paying governments astronomical sums for licences to operate 'third-generation' mobile services. In the UK five companies paid a total of £22.5 billion for licences. Vodafone was buying Mannesman, in a massive merger that followed not far behind Vodafone's 1999 acquisition of US company AirTouch. In the US WorldCom was trying to buy Sprint, SBC Communications had bought Ameritech, AT&T was buying MediaOne and Bell Atlantic had merged with GTE to form Verizon, all in mergers valued at over US$50 billion. It has been estimated that up to US$4 trillion was invested in telecommunications infrastructure over a period of four years, investment that in many cases proved of doubtful value and left the industry saddled with a huge debt burden.

The extreme 'new economy' euphoria that was present in the spring of 2000 was accompanied by many other markers of a major market top. The total market value of all US equities had reached approximately 180 per cent of US GDP, a similar relative magnitude to that reached at previous multi-year peaks in other markets that had been afflicted by extreme euphoria, such as Japan at the end of the 1980s and South-East Asia in the mid-1990s. AOL was combining with Time Warner in the ultimate 'TMT' merger. Microsoft and Intel had been admitted as components of the Dow Jones Industrial Average along with SBC Communications, although the committee responsible for the composition of the index resisted strong pressure from some quarters to include Cisco. In the UK the composition of the FTSE 100 index is mechanically related to companies' market capitalizations and therefore no discretion was possible. The rise and rise of the 'new economy' stocks meant that nine new economy stocks were admitted to the FTSE 100 right at the market peak, in March 2000. These companies – including Baltimore Technologies, Freeserve, Celltech and Psion – pushed out well-known 'old economy' names such as Whitbread and Hanson. At its peak the market capitalization of Baltimore Technologies reached over £4.5 billion, but by mid-2001 it had crashed to little more than £120 million.

Does the demise of the 'new economy' stocks and the accompanying massive bear market in equities mean that the whole idea of a new economy was just a myth, and that the many thousands of words that were written by so many about the implications of globalization, networking, scalability and 'internet economics' were so much claptrap? A full answer to this question is complicated and part of the rest of this book is concerned with elaborating upon and explaining some of the points that are here summarized briefly.

It is obviously not yet clear what will be the ultimate impact of the internet and the revolution in communications. As with other great developments and inventions such as the automobile, telephone and commercial air travel, it may be many years before the full effects on the way we live and on the economy are apparent. What we can say though is that, contrary to 'new era' beliefs, there has been no big increase in trend economic growth, certainly not globally and probably not even in the US, there is no guarantee that inflation is going to remain low, and that even if there was to be lower inflation and higher trend growth because of the developments in technology and communications, it would not have justified the huge re-rating of the US and other stock markets. In these respects the arguments made by the believers in the 'new economy' were wrong. This conclusion follows from the simple application of the basic logic of traditional economics and from the knowledge that we now have about the unsustainability of the 1995–2000 stock market gains.

One popular 'new era' argument was that the rise in productivity that the internet had supposedly made possible would result in a rise in profit share in the economy. This was self-evidently false and contradicted the other 'new economy' belief that the internet would hugely increase competition in the global economy and hence make price increases impossible. The internet sector itself was an example of the economics of perfect competition in reverse. In the perfect competition model of economics businesses are attracted to compete by super-normal profits being earned in an industry, and as new entrants come in to the industry those abnormal profits are competed away. In the internet industry there were no profits to begin with, only losses. New entrants came in at a rapid rate, attracted by the prospects of a quick stock market killing. Profits that were not even there in the first place were being competed for.

In the US economic statistics a sharp increase in investment was associated with an increase in the growth of labour productivity in the economy as a whole from 1995 onwards. However, this should not be expected to increase profit *share* because, in a competitive economy, the benefit from improvements in labour productivity should ultimately fall to labour itself, through higher real wages. That is, it is consumers rather than producers that will benefit. If labour productivity were to be higher without real wage rates being higher, then the extra profits available would encourage the employment of more labour, eventually pushing up real wages. Where it could, in theory, benefit is by increasing profit *growth*. Labour productivity growth is a key element of economic growth. If productivity growth is higher, then economic growth will be higher and therefore so will profits growth, even with profits maintaining a constant share of the growing economy. Higher prospective profits growth could, in theory, justify the stock market moving to a higher rating relative to current profits, a topic that is discussed in more detail in Chapter 4.

However, a significant rise in the trend growth rate of the US economy (that is the long-term sustainable growth rate of the economy) would be reflected to some extent in a somewhat higher trend growth rate for the industrialized world as a whole, because the US is the dominant economy. In addition, 'new economy' factors were supposed to be at work to some, more limited, extent in the European economies, providing an additional boost to global trend growth if the 'new paradigm' views were correct. Higher trend growth of the global economy should have been associated with a higher risk-free real rate of return (that is real interest rate), because economic theory suggests the prospective trend growth rate and the real interest rate should tend to be equal over time. But this is not what occurred from 1995 onwards, casting serious doubt on the idea that prospective long-term economic growth rates and profits growth had moved up to a higher level.

The equality between prospective real growth and the real interest rate is discussed in more depth in Chapter 4. For now it is sufficient to note that the real interest rate is a key element in the cost of capital and prospective real growth is a key component of the return on capital, so it makes sense that the two should be related because in equilibrium the cost of capital and the return on capital are supposed to be the same. In Figure 2.4 the global

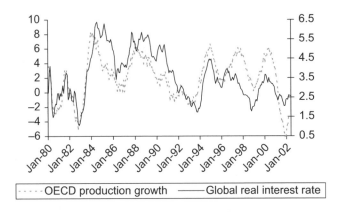

Figure 2.4 Global real interest rate and production growth

long-term real interest rate (in theory in a global capital market the risk-free real interest rate should be the same everywhere) is estimated by taking a weighted average of the measured long-term real interest rates in the five major economies. Each country's long-term real interest rate is calculated as the 10-year government bond yield minus a 3-year rolling average of the inflation rate. The chart shows that the ups and downs – the medium-term cycles – in this measure of the global real interest rate correlate fairly well with the upswings and downswings in global economic growth, measured here by using industrial production growth for the OECD (developed) economies. This is as should be expected and suggests that this measure of the global real interest rate is a credible one. (The true global real interest rate cannot really be observed in practice because the real interest rate as a concept is about the *expected* real return in the future and therefore requires an expected inflation rate to measure.)

The chart shows that far from rising significantly from 1995–96 in response to new growth prospects produced by the 'new economy', the global real interest rate actually fell, falling below the level that would have been expected given the rate of global economic growth. The investment share of US GDP was rising sharply at that time. The fall in the real interest rate could have been compatible with the rising investment share if both were being driven by a big rise in the savings rate. The problem is that the US savings rate had begun to fall steeply, on its way down to zero for the personal savings rate measure.

The fall in the real interest rate in fact is more suggestive of a fall in the trend rate of global economic growth, rather than a rise. Or, it could simply be the result of a massive excess of liquidity pushing up bond prices and lowering government bond yields (which are the basis for this measure of the real interest rate) below the level that is realistic in terms of the long-term fundamentals. Or, most likely, it could be both of these. Later in this book it is argued that it is often a falling away of the trend growth rate, combined with excessively loose monetary policy, that creates the economic circumstances that underlie an asset price mania.

What about the pick-up in productivity growth from 1995 that the US economic statistics do show as having occurred? There continues to be much debate about how genuine the apparent rise in productivity growth is, with some economists suspecting that it has more to do with the statistical methods used to measure productivity rather than any real change in the economy's long-run potential. In a widely quoted paper,[7] Professor Robert Gordon estimated that the rise in measured productivity growth could be accounted for by the normal effects of the economic cycle, statistical changes in the way that inflation is measured, and increasing productivity in the production of computers alone. He argued that outside the computer manufacturing industry there was no evidence for a general improvement in productivity growth. Other economists have disputed this and come up with different findings more supportive of the idea of a pick-up in the trend rate of productivity growth from 1995 onwards. However, three considerations that cast significant doubt on the idea that there has been any genuine improvement in productivity growth should be noted.

First, asset bubbles, if sustained for long enough, will inevitably tend to result in higher productivity growth, given the way productivity is measured from the national accounts statistics. During the Japanese bubble economy of the late 1980s productivity growth also appeared high until the bubble burst. The reason is that productivity is measured as the value added in production (that is the value of the output produced minus the cost of raw materials and components that were used in producing it) per employee involved in production, and per hour worked in the US system (that does not count an increase in the number of hours worked as an increase in productivity). This amounts to the same as the total of wages and salaries and profits per total hours worked. In an asset bubble that persists for years, more and more people will be working in areas that are directly or indirectly benefiting from the mania. Because returns from the mania are, by definition, so high, profits and salaries in these areas (for example fund management, investment banking) will also be high and therefore so will be their contribution to measured productivity. The US GDP statistics in fact show that from the mid-1990s onwards the finance (and real estate) sector of the US economy was a major contributor to the economy's accelerated growth, showing average growth in real terms of about 6 per cent annually.

Second, if economic growth is higher then measured productivity growth is going to be higher, even if these effects are only occurring as a result of the business cycle and not from any change in the long-term trend. Normally business cycle expansions are cut short by a rise in inflation that occurs when growth has persisted above trend for too long. It will be argued later in this book that the global dimension of the 1995–2000 financial asset mania contributed to suppressing inflation in the US, meaning that the business cycle expansion, and the accompanying cyclical upswing in productivity, was sustained for longer than would have been normal, making what was a cyclical phenomenon appear like a secular shift.

Third, the investment-driven nature of the expansion combined with the way the statistics are measured to create the statistical appearance of higher productivity growth. The US government statisticians use a technique known as 'hedonic' price measurement to take account of improvements in the quality of some categories of goods, particularly information technology. The basic idea is that it is wrong to treat a personal computer, for instance, purchased today as being the same thing as a personal computer purchased 10 years ago. The buyer today is getting much more for his money – more computing power – than 10 years ago, and this needs to be taken into account by downwardly adjusting the implicit price of today's computer, as measured in the statistics, relative to the price of the old computer. The effect of this adjustment will be to show more of today's spending on computers relative to previous years' spending as being an increase in volume –the volume of computing power – and consequently less as an increase in prices. Because computer prices have not been increasing much anyway, the actual effect is to show in the statistics a huge decline in prices over time and a huge increase in volumes. There are reasons to doubt whether this statistical treatment is appropriate, and these are discussed in Chapter 5 of this book.

Because the economic boom of the late 1990s was investment-driven, on the back of the financial asset mania, the hedonic price measurement approach, largely applying to investment goods, has a magnified effect in the national (GDP) accounts. Depreciation of capital equipment is not deducted in the calculation of GDP (*gross* domestic product). If, for instance, a company invests in computer hardware purchased from a computer manufacturer, then this will count as revenues (contributing to 'profits') for the manufacturer but it will not count as a cost for the company making the investment, at least not in the GDP accounts. GDP will be increased by the amount of the investment. If, compared with previous similar investments in computer hardware, hedonic measurement is being applied to calculate the implicit price of the computing power, then this will show up as an increase in the volume of GDP (real GDP) and a decrease in price (a fall in the deflator). If this sort of investment is playing a large role in driving GDP growth, then the result will be strong increases in real GDP, apparently strongly rising gross trading surpluses for the corporate sector, strong productivity growth and falling prices. It could be contended that the result is then merely determined by the statistical measurement process applied.

There have been plenty of studies designed to ascertain the existence and magnitude of any acceleration of the productivity trend of the US economy. The results of these types of studies, however sophisticated the methodology, are always going to be determined largely by the veracity and quality of statistics that the researcher has to work with. Given the factors noted above, and the fact that we now know that the behaviour of the US financial markets over 1995–2000 constituted a giant bubble, common sense – and economic logic – would suggest that there has not been any improvement in the underlying trend of productivity growth or of economic growth in the US economy. At least in this respect the 'new economy' was indeed a myth.

The 'True Economy'

The quote from Paul Volcker, Alan Greenspan's predecessor as Fed chairman, at the head of this chapter highlights how narrow (that is concentrated) the bull market in equities had become by 1999. This is one of the common features of mania. As a mania intensifies, it eventually becomes increasingly narrowly focused on the areas for which euphoria has been rationalized. Funds are sucked into these areas of the markets and of the economy, increasingly at the expense of other areas. By this stage of advanced mania, the bubble has become the driving force in the economy, allocating – that is misallocating – the economy's resources into the mania areas, and 'crowding out' the rest of the economy.

This pattern was very evident from 1998 onwards. For the US market, on some, very broad-based, measures the stock market entered a bear market from April 1998. In September 1999 Ned Davis Research estimated that the average stock in its database of more than 7,000 stocks had fallen by nearly 20 per cent from that date. Even within the large capitalization S&P 500, well over half of the capitalization was represented by just 50 stocks.

In the UK, and European markets, the issue of 'old economy' companies facing unreasonably depressed share prices and hence being denied equity financing had become a concern by late 1999. The *Financial Times* noted in February 2000 that textile company Courtaulds was trading on a price–earnings ratio of less than four ahead of a takeover approach, in an environment in which the valuation spreads between favoured and less favoured companies was exceptionally wide. The *Financial Times* also noted that 12 FTSE 100 stocks in the less favoured areas had seen their share prices plunge by 40 per cent or more over the preceding year. In the UK, and Europe, many smaller 'old economy' companies were choosing to leave the stock market, prompting the government in the UK to consider measures to help. Ironically, however, at the same time the government was also looking at how to treat share options granted by internet companies to their employees more favourably for tax purposes, showing a failure to understand the forces at work.

The same trends were present in the US markets in late 1999. In the mutual funds area they were manifested in heavy redemptions of value-oriented stock funds in favour of growth funds run by groups such as Janus and Vanguard. In the economy production of information processing equipment was exploding while production of 'low-tech' business equipment was contracting. There was plenty of anecdotal evidence of the technology mania negatively impacting other markets also. In the commodities business, major institutions such as J.P. Morgan and Merrill Lynch announced plans to close down their energy and/or commodity trading units.

The most obvious economic consequence of the technology mania was the huge rise in the investment share of GDP. As Figure 2.5 – showing private investment as a share of GDP, where both are expressed in real terms – indicates, this investment surge was unprecedented in modern times. Even when considered in nominal terms, to eliminate the problem of the probably flawed methodology used to estimate the price change of investment goods, the rise in investment share was considerable. At the time this was considered by most to be a good thing – the market's way of allocating resources to where the growth potential supposedly was, in order to maximize that potential. Unfortunately, as author Edward Chancellor[8] has noted, manias result in over-investment that in fact represents a misallocation of resources. Telecoms companies that made huge infrastructure investments are now bankrupt. The US$6 billion of capital in satellite telecommunications consortium Iridium, for example, was on the verge of literally going up in smoke in March 2000 when its 66 satellites were due to be pulled from orbit before being rescued at the last minute by the US government.

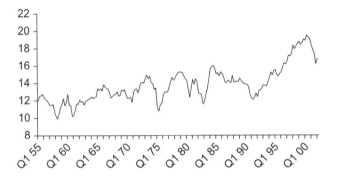

Figure 2.5 US real investment as % of GDP

Comparisons are now often being made between the US financial bubble and the Japanese bubble of the late 1980s. However, amongst the many very important differences between the two episodes, a crucial one is that Japan was (and still is) an economy with huge excess private savings. These excess savings have not been able to find adequate outlets domestically because Japan has been an overregulated economy with constrained opportunities for domestic investment. Instead Japanese savings have tended to be invested overseas, at least in part. In the 1980s this kept the yen weak and encouraged Japanese growth to be oriented towards the export sector of the economy, in a process that was ultimately unsustainable. The bubble – and the huge real estate investments it encouraged – can be seen to some extent as the markets' way of destroying the excess of savings, given the lack of genuine investment opportunities.

However, the US is a savings deficient economy and can little afford its relatively limited savings being misallocated in worthless investment projects. Worse still, the financial mania of the second half of the 1990s resulted directly in a sharp fall in the personal savings rate towards zero. This can be seen statistically in Figure 2.6, which explains the personal savings rate in terms of just two variables – stock market capitalization as a per cent of GDP and the short-term interest rate. If short-term interest rates are lower then the savings rate tends to be lower, but the driving force in the collapse of the savings rate in the late 1990s was the doubling of stock market capitalization relative to GDP during the giant bubble.

During the bull market two false and mutually inconsistent views about savings were common. One was that the equities bull market would inevitably go on because demographic factors determined that more and more people would be saving for their retirement. This view was

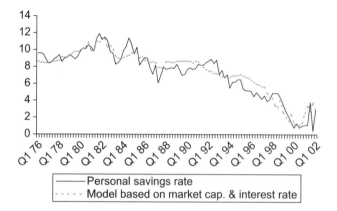

Figure 2.6 Model of US personal savings rate

theoretically, as well as empirically, false. In simple terms it is theoretically wrong because it would not be possible for a large chunk of the population to retire on elevated equity values. If a large part of the population were retiring trend economic growth would be slower and who would buy the equity being sold by pensioners except at much lower values? The view was empirically false because the savings rate was going down during the bull market. In the late stages the net buyers of equity were in fact companies as they increased their gearing through debt-financed acquisitions and stock buy-backs. The personal sector was a net seller of equities overall, despite the increase in margin debt and the flow of funds into highly speculative stocks such as the internet stocks. The US non-financial corporate sector was a net buyer of shares at an annual rate of over US$200 billion in 1998 and 1999.

The second widely held view was that the low US savings rate was really an illusion because it did not take into account the huge gains in stock market wealth that were being made. This argument involves a misunderstanding of the nature of savings. For the economy savings are the part of income that is not consumed and instead is invested in assets capable of generating future growth in income. An increase in stock market values is not savings and is not available for investment. It merely represents the market placing a higher value on existing assets. If people consider a rise in their stock portfolios to be a good substitute for savings – as they clearly did over 1995–2000 – then this is a problem because investment cannot exceed savings indefinitely. If the savings rate is low then the investment rate ultimately will also be low. Those analysts who appeared to believe both that demographic factors inevitably meant the powerful bull market in stocks would continue and that people did not need to save much because the stock market was going up were living in a fantasy world where wealth seemingly could be created magically out of nothing.

As it was, the mania encouraged a huge rise in investment and a sharp fall in private savings. By 2001 the total savings of the US personal and non-financial business sectors had fallen back to the levels of the early 1990s in *actual dollar amount*. For the private sector as a whole the gap between savings and investment (that is the private sector's financial deficit) was an unprecedented 7 per cent of GDP. Figure 2.7 places this in context for the personal and non-financial business sectors together (that is the bulk of the private sector). As can be seen, historically these two sectors together had not run a deficit (that is the line in the chart was always above zero) until 1997, from which time their financial balance plunged into huge deficit.

The US private sector financial deficit means that the US private sector is not saving enough to finance its own investment or, another way of looking at it, is consuming and investing more than its income. This deficit, of course,

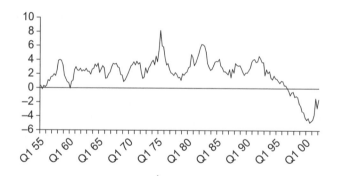

Figure 2.7 US personal and corporate financial balance as % GDP

had to be financed by the private sector selling financial assets or incurring financial liabilities. Given that we are talking about the private sector as a whole the net increase in these liabilities is necessarily either to the government or to the rest of the world. In the late 1990s many economists took solace from the fact that the US government was running a comfortable surplus. If you took these government savings into account, the argument went, then the total savings picture for the country as a whole did not look quite as bad. What was wrong with this argument was that the government was also benefiting from the stock market bubble, in indirect ways that went beyond the revenues deriving from capital gains tax. This is difficult to pinpoint, but it is apparent both from statistical analysis and from the fact that as the US stock market bubble has been deflating the US government's accounts have been deteriorating by more than can be accounted for by tax and spending changes alone.

The huge increase in the corporate sector's financial deficit in the late 1990s correlates well with the sharp widening of credit spreads (that is the difference between corporate bond yields and government bond yields) that occurred from that time. For example the yield on corporate bonds rated BAA exceeded that on government debt by around 1.5 percentage points over most of the period from 1994 to 1997. By the end of 2000 this spread had blown out to around 3.0 per cent. Although other explanations are possible this strongly suggests that the financing burden on the economy represented by the financial deficit of the corporate sector in particular, but also of the private sector as a whole, was a source of market stress by the time the equity bull market peaked. Another manifestation of the lack of savings in the US has been the widely discussed enormous build-up of debt within the economy. There are a variety of measures of total debt and consequently a number of different estimates, but most measures of total private debt show it as having reached a level equivalent to roughly one-and-a-half times GDP by 2000, compared with about equal to GDP at the beginning of the secular bull market in the early 1980s.

The main way that the US private sector financial deficit overall has been financed is from the huge net inflow of capital from overseas, that is the US current account deficit. This has reached around 5 per cent of GDP on an annual basis, and by late 2002 was showing little sign of improvement. A current account deficit of this size would be large for a normal economy but for the US its financing represents a huge claim on the rest of the world's net savings.

The current account deficit can be shown to have been a function of the US financial bubble with a statistical model illustrated in Figure 2.8. In this model the behaviour of the current account is explained very well using only three economic variables – stock market capitalization as a per cent of GDP (the key influence on the savings rate as shown before), the dollar's exchange rate against other currencies on a trade-weighted basis, and US domestic demand growth. Because the stock market capitalization is a key variable the blowing out of the current account deficit is seen clearly to be a manifestation of the financial bubble.

By late 2002 the sharp fall in private investment that accompanied the equity bear market meant that the corporate sector's deficit had been corrected to a significant degree, although it is doubtful that this correction is yet sufficient. The personal sector deficit has also improved slightly but the personal sector remains a long way from its historic large surpluses. The government's accounts have deteriorated sharply. But looking at these individual macro-sectors of the economy is not particularly helpful to understanding the stage of unwinding of the bubble that has been reached. For this the important marker is the current account deficit because this shows the deficiency of savings for the economy as a whole. The model underlying the chart allows for an infinite number of possible outcomes because the current account is explained by three separate factors. However, it

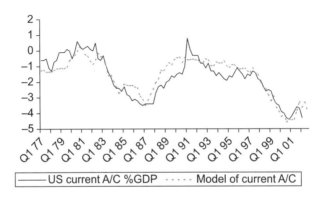

Figure 2.8 Model of US current account

suggests that an even greater decline in the stock market than has already been seen, or a severe recession in the economy, or a major fall in the dollar (in excess of 30 per cent), or more likely a combination of all of these will be necessary before the current account of the balance of payments is brought back towards balance.

The conclusion from this is that the financial bubble is still with us – and the US remains a 'bubble economy' – until these events have been seen, most notably a very sharp fall in the dollar. The vestiges of the mania remain in the stock market while the full force of the bubble has been transferred to the government bond markets. The next chapters will show that the forces still holding up this giant bubble are a large monetary excess and the global, and institutional, nature of the mania, which has left the rest of the world with an irrational attachment to the US dollar. The markets' belief in the 'new economy' has already been discredited. By the time the greatest financial bubble ever experienced has fully collapsed – which could take several years – the investment industry is likely to look quite different. Investors' other cherished beliefs – such as the idea that in a global economy inflation will never be a problem – will have also been shaken.

CHAPTER 3

Cyclical Bubbles and Structural Bubbles

Monetary Cycles and Liquidity Indicators

Sustained rises in asset prices beyond the long-run trend (when adjusted for inflation) usually have their origin in expansive monetary conditions. The acceleration in the US equities bull market from 1995–96 was no exception, and coincided with an aggressive loosening of monetary policy in the US and the other major economies that began in 1995. This monetary stimulus by the major central banks was originally put in place in response to a slowdown of the global economy in 1995.

Technically, in monetary economics, loose monetary conditions occur when the quantity of money in the economy (that is the total of bank deposits and cash currency), known as the money supply, exceeds the demand for it, relative to the demand for other assets such as shares, bonds or real estate. The growth of the supply of money is controlled or influenced by the central bank, via its monetary policy that is observable in its setting of the key short-term interest rate. It is also closely associated with increases in credit demand because credit extension by banks (that is lending) involves the creation of new bank deposits (that is money). But money created in this way can expand more than the demand to hold it within the economy. In simple terms this is because those borrowing from the banks are usually borrowing funds they require to use (for example to buy a house), and the recipients of those funds (that is bank deposits) may not wish to hold their wealth all in the form of money. They may want to put some into stocks or bonds or other assets. If the amount of money created in the economy exceeds the amount that individuals and businesses wish to hold (as cash or bank deposits) then monetary conditions are loose and, by definition, there will be demand for other financial and real assets and/or goods and services.

For the economy as a whole an 'excess' of money cannot be eliminated in the first instance by being used to purchase other assets. For every buyer there is a seller and therefore sellers of assets, such as shares, will be holding the money. But this process tends to raise asset prices. If expansionary monetary conditions are prolonged then spending on goods and services will also tend to increase and eventually this could stimulate increases in goods and services' prices, meaning inflation. In the end, assuming no reversal of course by the central bank, an expansionary monetary policy will be 'neutralized' by inflation. Once prices have risen enough the available quantity of money will not be excessive because a greater amount of money will be required for transactions, because real estate and all other prices will be higher. Inflation erodes the value of money in real terms and makes the greater quantity of money again appropriate for the economy.

If, in response to an expansion of the money supply greater than the demand for money, prices of goods and services and all other asset prices rise together, then the excess of money is quickly eliminated and, by definition, there would be no real terms increase in asset prices. Stock prices would have risen, but only by the same amount as other prices. In economic theory this outcome would be the result of 'rational expectations'. In practice, the prices of goods and services are more 'sticky' than, for instance, stock prices and it makes sense to believe that equity prices will move up well before any generalized inflation in the event of a sustained monetary expansion. Classically, therefore, the domestic investor is supposed to do well in the stock market if the central bank is implementing a loose monetary policy, particularly in its early stages. But for the global investor, who is comparing the performance of financial assets in different national markets, the key will be the reaction of the currency to loose monetary policy. Economic textbooks quite reasonably teach that a loosening of monetary policy, other things being equal, will cause a depreciation of the currency relative to foreign currencies. There are a number of ways of looking at this. If there is an excess of money domestically then some of this excess money is likely to find its way into foreign assets as much as domestic assets, causing a weakening of the currency. Looser money – in the earlier stages of the business cycle – tends to be associated with lower interest rates. If interest rates are lowered but foreign rates remain unchanged, then this also calls for a depreciation of the currency, because a lower value of the currency will be necessary to encourage foreign investors to hold it – with the hope of a future appreciation – to compensate for the lower interest return.

If the central bank loosens monetary policy and the stock market goes up in response but the currency goes down equivalently then the foreign, or global, investor in the market is no better off. His gains on the stock market have been offset by currency losses. In terms of monetary economic theory, this situation will arise if the 'real exchange rate' is tending to remain stable. The real exchange rate is the inflation-adjusted exchange rate, a measure of competitiveness that takes into account movements of the currency and changes in price levels relative to price levels in trading partners of the country. If the value of a country's currency falls on the foreign exchange markets but prices are rising faster than in trading partners by an equivalent amount, then there is no improvement in the country's competitiveness. The depreciation of the currency is offset by inflation and there is no change in the 'real exchange rate'.

In the classical example of the central bank monetary policy loosening, both the consequent rise in the stock market and the depreciation of the currency are in fact symptoms of inflation, where inflation correctly should be considered as a fall in the value of money. The fall in the value of money arising from the monetary excess created by the central bank policy does not manifest immediately in goods and services prices, because these are sticky, but it does manifest in a fall in the value of money relative to stocks (that is higher stock prices) and a fall in the value of the domestic money from the point of view of foreigners (that is a depreciation of the currency). What the foreign investor wants to see is not a situation where the currency immediately reflects the inflationary implications of the monetary excess (that is where the real exchange rate is tending to remain stable) but a situation where the currency remains resilient to the incipient inflation (that is the real exchange rate is tending to rise). In the latter case the equity market should – in theory at least – tend to out-perform other markets when measured in a common currency.

In a traditional cyclical upturn, the first sign of impending economic recovery is a loosening of monetary conditions by the central bank, classically manifested in lower short-term interest rates, a steeper spread between long-term and short-term government bond yields (that is a steeper yield curve), and a rise in money supply growth. Stock prices tend to rise and the currency – according to conventional theory – should depreciate. If the loosening of monetary policy is prolonged, economic activity should pick up as the demand for goods and services rises because of monetary excess, and there is a perception that wealth has increased because of higher asset prices. Eventually there should be inflation of goods and services prices. The central bank at some stage tightens policy – that is it increases interest rates – in order to combat inflation, given that economic activity is by then strong. Interest rates are increased, and in the end – particularly as by this late stage of the cycle inflation is already eroding real purchasing power in the economy – this will provoke an economic downturn, or recession, which is preceded by a decline in equity prices.

Late in the cycle it is never easy for the central bank to know if interest rates have been increased enough to bring inflation under control or, conversely, have been increased too much so as to bring about an unnecessarily deep recession. The longer a business expansion goes on, and the stronger it is, the higher short-term interest rates (adjusted for inflation) are likely to have to go in order to moderate growth and bring inflation under control. This is because the longer and stronger the expansion, the more the economy's production capacity will be strained and the stronger property prices will tend to become, and therefore the stronger the demand for credit will be. A greater tightening of monetary policy – viewed in terms of interest rates – will be necessary in order to 'choke off' the surging demand for bank credit. A very rough 'rule of thumb' for the western industrialized economies (most of which have been capable of achieving economic growth of 2.0–2.5 per cent annually over the long term) is that a short-term interest rate of 2.5–3.0 per cent in real terms has been appropriate for an economy growing roughly at its trend (that is the short-term interest rate minus the expectation for annualized inflation should be 2.5–3.0 per cent), but a substantially higher rate in the broad range 3.5–6.0 per cent in real terms has been appropriate in the advanced stages of an economic boom. For an economy in recession a real rate below 1 per cent, perhaps as low as 0 per cent or slightly negative (that is an interest rate below the rate of inflation), could well be appropriate. More sophisticated interest rate rules, such as the 'Taylor Rule', seek to estimate the appropriate, or 'neutral', short-term interest rate more exactly using the inflation rate and the degree of unused capacity in the economy.

In terms of conventional monetary theory, the right interest rate in an economic boom when inflation is rising is one that brings the rate of monetary growth down and under control. The problem is that in today's global, and largely financially deregulated, economy what constitutes an appropriate measure of money supply is difficult to define. The boundary between money and substitutes for money is blurred, and the demand for money can also swing around as a result of influences from the global financial markets. For example, in a global bull market in bonds that causes bond yields in a particular country to decline by more than might be justified by inflation performance, residents may wish to hold more of their wealth in bank deposits (that is an increase in the demand for money) because yields on bonds appear unattractive. Over 2001–02 the European Central Bank argued that the severe bear market in equities globally was boosting demand for money in the Eurozone, because Eurozone residents were increasingly preferring to hold money in preference to equities.

These, and other, reasons have caused central banks, most economists and other observers to abandon money supply as an economic indicator that has any meaning. Of the major central banks only the European Central Bank retains money supply at the core of its monetary policy framework, and it has been widely criticized for doing so. This shift in the general climate of opinion – which viewed money supply as an indicator of major importance in the early 1980s but now sees it as having no value whatsoever – is, in time, likely to be viewed as an important part of the background that enabled the policy mistakes of the 1990s to be made.

For the fact is that, shortcomings notwithstanding, the highly stimulative monetary policy that provided the environment conducive to the formation of the giant asset bubble in the US shows up very clearly in the behaviour of money supply, behaviour that is also mirrored, to a lesser extent, in the other western economies.

Figure 3.1 shows that a surge in the rate of growth of the broad money supply measure M3 from the mid-1990s returned money growth close to the rates that had been typical for much of the inflationary 1970s. This money growth surge coincided more or less exactly with the growing bubble in the US asset markets.

Given the shortcomings of straightforward monetary aggregates as measures of monetary conditions, it is possible to create superior monetary measures (liquidity indicators) by combining money supply growth together with other relevant indicators such as interest rate spreads (the slope of the yield curve) and real short-term interest rates together in one indicator. The exchange rate is also often used in this type of liquidity indicator, although the inclusion of the exchange rate is suspect in theory because real exchange rates can fluctuate for reasons other than related to monetary conditions (for example changes in fiscal policy), and fluctuations that do have their origins in monetary conditions can better be picked up by the other indicators. In Figure 3.2 a relatively simple liquidity indicator for the US is calculated using only M3 money supply growth in real terms (that is adjusted for inflation) and short-term interest rates in real terms (deflated using a three-year rolling average of inflation). These two different components (money supply and interest rates) are combined by representing each in terms of

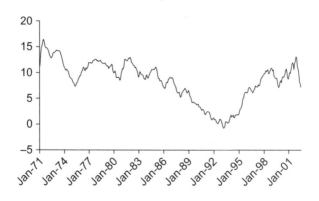

Figure 3.1   US money supply (M3) growth

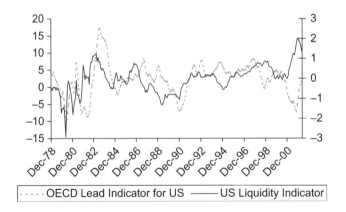

Figure 3.2   US liquidity indicator

standard deviations from the average over the whole period (that is standardizing), and then averaging the two standardized series. In the chart the resulting liquidity indicator is compared with the OECD's leading indicator for the US economy, itself an advance indicator of industrial production growth. The liquidity indicator moves well in advance of the OECD's indicator, showing that it is a very early indicator of the economic cycle, as a good liquidity indicator should be.

The key point to note from this chart is that from 1995 the US liquidity indicator began a gradual and sustained rise that by the end of 1998 had taken it to an historically high level, exceeded (on the chart) only by the extent of liquidity ease in late 1982, right at the beginning of the secular bull market in equities and the long economic expansion of the 1980s. After dipping down in 1999, the liquidity indicator rose strongly again to reach easily all time record levels at the end of 2001, suggesting extraordinary looseness of monetary policy at that time.

In a global financial market, as far as understanding financial market developments is concerned, it can make more sense to consider a 'global' measure of liquidity. In Figure 3.3 such a 'global' indicator is estimated by calculating liquidity indicators for the Eurozone, Japan and the UK in exactly the same way as described for the US, above, and then taking a weighted average (using GDP weights) of the US, Eurozone, Japan and UK indicators. The global liquidity indicator is compared in the chart with the behaviour of global stock markets, as represented by the year-on-year change in the Morgan Stanley Capital International World Index. It can be seen that there is a good relationship, with the broad cycles in the stock market corresponding with the discernible cycles in liquidity.

The chart shows the same general pattern in liquidity conditions as for the US indicator alone. It should be borne in mind that over the whole period

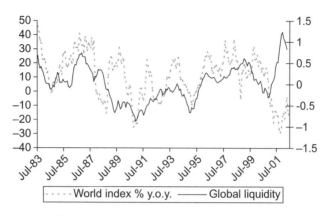

Figure 3.3 Global liquidity and stock markets

illustrated in the chart global equities were in a secular bull market so that the annual rate of appreciation of the world index (left scale) averages a high rate throughout. The annual capital return on the world market is sustained at a high level for most of the period from late 1995 through 2000. It is very noticeable that, beginning in 2001, stock market behaviour appeared to divorce itself completely from the liquidity cycle. While global liquidity surged to reach a record degree of monetary ease by the end of 2001, the global stock market became increasingly depressed throughout 2001 and 2002. The relationship between liquidity and the equities markets appears almost to have undergone a step shift at the beginning of 2001.

A 'Structural Bubble'

A 'cyclical bubble' can be thought of as developing if a rise in stock prices resulting from an expansive monetary policy goes beyond that which can be explained by the ensuing upturn in economic activity and ultimate inflation. A monetary expansion should ultimately give rise to a broad increase in all prices, for assets as well as goods and services, at least in theory. Because goods and services prices are sticky, traditional monetary economics suggests that a cyclical upturn in demand in the economy will be part of this process. If the rise in stock prices exceeds that which would be justified by the subsequent cyclical upturn in demand, output and profits and the eventual rise in prices, then it could be considered to be a cyclical bubble in the stock market. By definition, given that the rise in stock prices has gone beyond that which can be justified even from consideration of the cycle, a later bear market, in which prices fall back at least to fair value levels, is then inevitable.

Given the trend-following nature of a lot of investment today (discussed in its various forms in Chapter 6) any cyclical rise in asset prices would be likely to develop into a cyclical bubble of a greater or lesser magnitude. As the rise in asset prices encourages expectations of further asset appreciation, credit demand will tend to strengthen, leading to higher money growth if the central bank remains passive. Classically, it takes a central bank tightening to 'prick' the bubble, and this tightening is likely to have to be aggressive because the neutral short-term interest rate rises as the bubble gathers momentum. Then, the asset prices fall back very quickly because liquidity support for the market is taken away, and once the downtrend is established the neutral short-term interest rate falls sharply as speculative credit demand evaporates. Unless the central bank then cuts rates very rapidly, liquidity will tighten sharply. Trend-following behaviour by investors will act to speed the asset price decline, which will consequently be more violent than the preceding rise.

A 'structural bubble' is very different. In a structural bubble an above-trend rise in asset prices persists for so long that the structure of the economy is affected, and altered by the prolonged appreciation of asset prices and the expectation that high returns from the assets will continue. As an extreme example we can think of the pure pyramid (or 'Ponzi') scheme, such as that which dominated the Albanian economy in 1996–97. In a pure pyramid scheme, investors' accounts in the scheme are credited with unrealistic returns and if they demand payment, they can be paid out with funds contributed by other investors and newcomers. As with the principle of a chain letter, as long as the scheme continues to attract an ever-greater number of participants it appears viable. Investors in effect believe they are earning a high return on investment when all that is really going on within the pyramid is transfers of capital between the participants. If, hypothetically, we imagine such a pyramid growing to encompass virtually the whole economy (much as happened in Albania) then the fees that the scheme generates will become significant within the economy. Many people will be employed in various institutions administering the scheme and in ancillary services to those institutions. The fees – probably hidden – paid by the participants will be a significant part of consumer spending. A substantial part of investment may be oriented to infrastructure related to the growth of the 'Ponzi' scheme. Because the returns on investment in the pyramid-related activities appear so high, other avenues or opportunities for investment will be 'crowded out'.

For a pyramid scheme like this to keep on growing and growing to the point that its influence on the economy becomes pervasive probably requires three conditions to be fulfilled.

First, the central bank's monetary policy needs to be permissive, at least initially. People will believe that their wealth is increasing vastly. Together with loose money this will mean that consumer spending growth and the overall economy will tend to be strong, eventually producing inflationary pressures. If the pyramid keeps on growing it must be the case that either the central bank permits this rise in inflation or, for some reason or by some mechanism, incipient inflationary pressures are suppressed.

Second, and somewhat related to the first condition, the external value of the currency needs to remain relatively resilient. Because consumption will be strong, the trade account will be deteriorating, and with loose money classically the currency would be expected to be depreciating. If this were to happen it would be more likely to place a constraint on the bubble's dynamics, if only by facilitating the incipient rise in inflation. In an open economy, the most obvious way for the currency to be supported is if foreigners also participate in the pyramid. Capital flows are then supportive of the currency and contribute to the bubble process, rather than providing a constraint on the process.

Third, a giant pyramid scheme, or any process that creates a structural bubble, is more likely to take root if the authorities lend credibility in some way, either through active government involvement or implicit government or central bank support for, or sanctioning of, the scheme. Pyramid schemes that have existed in the past in developing countries such as Albania or Thailand have generally had backing from people in positions of authority. Without this, it is hard for the pyramid to carry the trust of the participants for long enough to become rooted in the structure of the economy.

Pure pyramid schemes, like chain letters, must come to an end eventually because at some point the funds credited to individuals' accounts within the scheme become so vast that withdrawals cannot be covered from the initial capital contributed by participants. At this point the pyramid is in danger of collapse if there is a loss of confidence and all the participants try to withdraw the funds to their account in the scheme. But the end may not come that quickly if the pyramid is by then integral to the structure of the economy. Precisely because it is part of the economy – employing people and with a broad range of mechanisms to draw in savings – it may initially be fairly resilient, with a reservoir of investors' trust and goodwill. Then the unravelling of the pyramid may take place over a prolonged period, tending to gather pace as it goes on. But once it starts, this unwinding is a process that cannot be halted.

When a structural bubble unwinds in this way it will clearly be associated with, possibly severe, economic weakness. Those who had been employed in the 'bubble activities' will lose their jobs. Investment in the supportive infrastructure will be redundant. Participant investors will recognize that wealth they believed they had was illusory. They will have to raise their savings rate to compensate. Credit demand – which in the later stages of the mania will have become very strong because of the strength of the economy and the speculative opportunities seemingly created – will collapse. The real short-term interest rate appropriate to any given central bank monetary stance will therefore be much lower. If the central bank does not cut interest rates dramatically money supply growth will be liable to fall sharply.

The process of the creation of the structural bubble is inflationary, because it is initially associated with an excessively lax monetary policy and a consequent economic boom. The dismantling of the bubble would be expected to be deflationary because the collapse of credit demand tends to lead to monetary contraction, eliminating any previous monetary excess and replacing it with a monetary deficiency. The most obvious example of this is the persistent deflation in Japan following the bursting of the structural bubble that built up in that economy in the late 1980s. But what if the central bank responds very promptly to the bursting of the bubble by slashing interest rates to an extent that money supply growth is maintained at a reasonable rate and a monetary contraction is avoided?

Theoretically, the prevention of a credit contraction would require that the central bank cut interest rates enough to allow banks to maintain asset growth, including lending to 'non-bubble' activities on a great enough scale to offset contraction in bubble-related areas. This would require that investment take place in the non-bubble sectors, including previously displaced investment being 'crowded in'. A major decline in the value of the currency must be part of this process for a number of related reasons: first, from a monetary perspective a marked loosening of monetary conditions occurs against a background of the economy tending to weaken (as the bubble implodes). This combination implies a weak currency. If the asset bubble has itself provided support to the currency because foreign capital has been attracted by the apparently high returns, then the currency decline should be even more severe. Second, a decline in the value of the currency to an under-valued level (that is a fall in the real exchange rate) is likely to be a necessary part of the process whereby new investment can be encouraged – in this case in the export and import substitution parts of the economy. Third, and related to this, the bursting of the asset bubble will mean that the savings of the private sector will need to be rebuilt. This implies weaker consumption than incomes, and this can only happen without severe economic weakness if either the government's fiscal policy becomes extremely stimulative, or if the current account of the balance of payments improves substantially (that is exports grow much more than imports). The latter, in turn, again requires a weak currency.

At first sight the process of unwinding of the 1980s Japanese bubble that has been taking place since 1990 does not seem to fit this model because the yen has not been particularly weak. However, two points should be noted: first, Japan has had a huge structural savings surplus which was not eliminated by the bubble and has left Japan with an unsustainably high level of net foreign assets in relation to the size of its economy. Ordinarily, this would tend to make the yen a very overvalued currency. The fact that it has not been overvalued as the asset bubble has unwound implies that the unwinding process has been a force keeping the currency weaker than it would otherwise have been. Second, Japan's central bank never eased monetary policy aggressively enough in the early stages of the bubble-burst to maintain credit and money growth. Credit has been contracting and the economy has been in a deflation. Therefore the Japan case is not an appropriate example for the discussion here, because the central bank did not act to maintain liquidity. For the same reason, neither is the unwinding of the 1920s bubble following the 1929 Wall Street crash a relevant example, because there was also a subsequent monetary contraction. In fact, there is no clear example of a central bank easing enough in the wake of the bursting of a structural bubble to maintain liquidity in the economy at a high level, that is, possibly, until the example that is the topic of this book.

The answer to the question posed is that if the central bank can successfully maintain money and credit growth as a structural asset bubble unwinds, then, in theory at least, the unwinding process must ultimately be associated with inflation. If money and credit growth are broadly maintained it implies that demand growth in the economy is supported, while the structural bubble has involved some wastage of the economy's resources meaning that, contrary to a common view, there is no overhang of excess capacity. The asset bubble begins from a monetary excess – by definition – although its momentum eventually gives it a life of its own. As the bubble unwinds, reversing the process that built it, the monetary excess will disappear as credit contracts, for as long as the central bank remains passive. But if the central bank does not remain passive, but is instead able to act aggressively enough to keep money and credit growth going then, logically, the monetary excess must remain. This must sooner or later be a source of inflation, and given that the unwinding process must then involve the currency being weak, it is easy to see how inflation in the economy is accommodated.

Conventional wisdom – seemingly shared by virtually all commentators on the subject – is that the bursting of an asset bubble must be deflationary. Some economists even go so far as to argue that excessively loose monetary policy is deflationary because it leads to the formation of asset bubbles that ultimately burst. These arguments are easy to understand because the bursting of an asset bubble is itself a force for, possibly severe, economic weakness. However, they can only be true if the bubble unwinding is associated with monetary contraction (as it generally has been in history).

Those who believe that a bursting asset bubble will lead to deflation even when there is no monetary contraction must explain why the relationship between the money supply and the economy has permanently shifted. In this case there is a monetary excess – in terms of the pre-bubble position – and deflation would create an even bigger excess, because prices would be falling. For this to be sustainable, there must by definition have been a big increase in the demand for money relative to the pre-bubble position. There is no adequate explanation of why the formation and unwinding of an asset bubble should have as its legacy a permanently higher demand for money than prior to the bubble. This is discussed further later in this chapter and in much more depth in Chapter 5, on 'Inflation or Deflation?'

Turning to the present-day US economy, the earlier chart on the US liquidity indicator shows the indicator surging to a record by late 2001, even as the stock market bubble unwound. The monetary easing by the US Federal Reserve was exceptionally aggressive, as it acted pre-emptively to support the economy in the wake of the severe equities bear market. The key short-term interest rate, the federal funds rate, was cut 11 times between January 2001 and December 2001, bringing it down from 6.5 per cent to a 40 year low of 1.75 per cent. The Fed's action was mirrored by a less pronounced easing in the other major western economies, with both the European Central Bank and the Bank of England cutting rates to historically low levels.

The chart on the global liquidity indicator and the annual change of the world stock market index showed that the extraordinarily large easing of global liquidity conditions was not reflected in strong global stock market performance. On the contrary, world stock markets remained entrenched in the severe bear market that began in 2000. During the secular bull market equities performed better than might have been predicted purely from the liquidity cycle – particularly in the bubble years of 1995–2000. During the bear market, as the bubble has unwound, they have been performing much worse. One interpretation of the relationship in the chart is that causation has been reversed since 2000. Whereas in the past the cycle of monetary conditions influenced the behaviour of the equities markets, since 2000 the liquidity cycle is being determined by central bank policies that are hostage to the financial markets. Central banks are being forced to keep monetary policy as easy as it needs to be to prevent a rapid and economically damaging implosion of the asset bubble.

Earlier it was explained that the bursting of a structural asset bubble must be accompanied by a weaker currency, particularly if the central bank takes aggressive monetary action in an attempt to forestall negative consequences for the economy. If this is true why, if the US has been experiencing the unwinding of a structural bubble, has the dollar – at least at the time of writing – not been particularly weak? There are two parts to the answer to this question. The first is that the asset bubble that began in 1995 was not merely a US phenomenon. It was a global bubble, albeit that the US led the way and the stock market mania was much more acute in the US than elsewhere. The second point is that the degree to which the asset bubble has unwound at the end of 2002, even in the US, is comparatively small in relation to the scale of the bubble.

This second point may seem unreasonable given that the years 2000–02 have witnessed one of the most severe equities bear markets in US history. However, the financial asset bubble has not merely been an equities bubble but also a bubble in debt. Government bonds, in particular, have become grossly overvalued in the years up to 2002, as explored more fully in the following chapter. The institutional structure in place to channel savings to financial assets operates in bonds as well as equities. The years 2000–02 to some extent have seen the bubble previously in equities transfer to the bond markets.

Furthermore, even as far as equities markets are concerned, at the end of 2002 there is still a long way to go before the bubble is fully unwound. A full unwinding inevitably must mean a return to the stock market levels that existed before the bubble began to form – that is the levels that the indices were at in 1995 (at least in the absence of major inflation). Asset manias, while they are occurring, appear to be about the creation of wealth, but in fact they are associated with the destruction of wealth, particularly if the illusory paper wealth gains discourage saving, as was the case in the US over 1995–2000. As was noted in the previous chapter, by 2001 the personal and non-financial business sectors' total savings in nominal terms (that is the dollar amount of savings) had fallen back to the level of 10 years previously. The limited amount of savings, and possibly more than the limited amount of savings, is invested in a way that only makes sense because of the existence of the asset bubble. Once the bubble is burst this investment is redundant and wealth is lower than at the starting point, justifying a falling back in asset prices at least to the levels where the bubble began to form.

Additionally, in late 2002 the out-performance of the US stock market relative to the other major stock markets, which was one of the symptoms of the bubble, has barely begun to be reversed. Figure 3.4 illustrates one example, of the out-performance of the S&P 500 relative to the UK FTSE 100, where both are expressed in a common currency. Given that barely a dent has been made in the long period of out-performance of the US markets relative to other global stock markets it is perhaps not surprising that the dollar has remained resilient. The chart in Figure 3.5 shows that, in real trade-weighted terms (that is measured against the currencies of trading partners and adjusted for relative inflation performance), by the end of 2001 the dollar had returned close to the grossly overvalued levels that it reached in the 'dollar mania' of the first half of

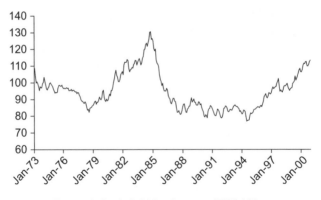

Figure 3.4   S&P 500 relative to FTSE 100

Figure 3.5   Real trade-weighted dollar

the1980s. A full bursting of the US asset bubble will involve a complete reversal of the dollar's rise from 1995–2001 at a very minimum.

The Structural Bubble and the Demand for Money

One of the features of the global bubble environment of the late 1990s was that it saw the economic orthodoxy of the 1980s era completely reversed. One of the lessons of the high inflation of the 1970s was that 'money matters'. That monetary policy should not accommodate commodity price shocks, such as an oil shock, because if it does it risks ratifying higher infla- tion expectations, was a key lesson. But by the late 1990s in most econo- mists' eyes money supply was discredited as a target or guide for monetary policy. The European Central Bank (ECB) was widely criticized, including by the IMF, for paying attention to money supply growth in setting its policy. As an economist at ABN-Amro bank put it, 'Only hard-line monetarists at the Bundesbank believe M3 has policy implications.'

By the late 1990s oil price hikes were widely believed to be 'disinflationary' or deflationary because of their effect in cutting purchasing power, thereby justifying interest rate cuts. The Fed itself used a sharp rise in oil prices as one of the reasons for cutting rates in February 2001, saying in its accompanying statement to explain the move, 'Consumer and business confidence has eroded further, exacerbated by rising energy costs that continue to drain consumer purchasing power and press on business profit margins.' Also interest rate reductions were believed to result in currency appreciation rather than depreciation. Routinely during 2000 and 2001 analysts explained the strength of the dollar and weakness of the euro in terms of the Fed being quicker to reduce rates in the face of economic weakness, and slower to raise rates, than the European Central Bank. The ECB's aversion to loose monetary policy was believed to retard growth in Europe thereby weakening the euro. In early 2000 weakness of the euro was being attributed by analysts to 'concern that the European Central Bank might be excessively aggressive in raising interest rates' (*Financial Times*, 26 January 2000). In March 2001 the *Financial Times* commented, 'It is precisely the ECB's reluctance to cut interest rates this year that has weighed on the euro.' (27 March 2001). This same sentiment was echoed in numerous items of financial market research. The flip side was that aggressive Fed rate cuts at that time were welcomed by foreign exchange strategists as unambiguously bullish for the dollar, despite the weakening US economy. A typical comment from one senior investment executive, in March 2001, was as follows: 'My view is that aggressive rate cuts when the economy is slowing down is actually good for a currency.'

The thinking behind this new orthodoxy was articulated by Bank of England Monetary Policy Committee member DeAnne Julius in 1999: 'We are moving away from the model of the economy where pressures of the labour market would allow wage increases which in turn would develop into price increases. We're moving to one where international competitive pressures are responsible for price-setting and the amount of wage increases that can be afforded are derived from prices that producers have to meet in order to sell their product.' In other words, inflation for any one economy is not determined domestically but globally, and because of international competitive pressures cannot be high. In this world, the main impact of monetary policy is on growth and loose money will result in strong economic growth that, by attracting capital from overseas, will result in a strong currency. Shocks affecting corporate costs, such as an oil price hike, will squeeze profits and weaken growth, demanding looser monetary policy to combat.

This was the perspective from which most financial economists and commentators were viewing the world in the late 1990s and into the beginning of the new century. But this reversal of the principles of conventional monetary economics will ultimately be seen to have been a function of the financial bubble environment, just as the new economy theories proved to be. The principles of orthodox monetary economics are based on logical conclusions that derive from the starting assumptions of rationality on the part of the participants in the economy. An asset bubble, by definition, occurs in defiance of the principle of the narrowly based definition of economic rationality. Therefore an asset bubble will likely see the development of its own internal logic, which, as long as it is to exist, must be the logic to which the participants subscribe. However, ultimately the logic of the bubble is only a special case, and the conventional relationships must reassert themselves.

One justification offered for the notion that if a central bank cuts interest rates its currency should strengthen is that in the modern world capital flows have come to overwhelm trade in goods and services in importance, and within capital flows portfolio investment in equities and bonds has increased enormously in importance. Then, the argument goes, reductions in interest rates are positive for the currency because they will encourage capital flows into the, now more attractive, domestic equity and bond markets. This argument really only holds good in a bubble environment because the implicit assumption is that rises in stock and bond markets will develop into a trend, once begun. Otherwise, in theory the adjustment in the valuations of stock and bond markets to lower interest rates is a one-off adjustment which, when complete, leaves the prospective return on stocks and bonds lower than before (in line with cash, which now carries a lower interest rate) and therefore demands a *lower* external value of the currency. This is because foreign investors will require the prospect of currency appreciation – which is more likely from the lower levels of the currency – to keep them invested.

As explained previously, a rise in financial markets that takes on its own momentum (a cyclical bubble or a structural bubble) must begin from a 'monetary excess'. There is an excessive supply of money relative to wealth that investors wish to hold in the form of money, meaning that there is demand for other financial assets such as stocks and bonds. In this sense, money (meaning, largely, bank deposits) is a substitute for other financial assets. A cyclical rise in financial asset prices, possibly turning into a bubble, can develop because prices of goods and services do not rise, at least initially, in line with financial asset prices. Also as explained earlier, if this then develops into a structural bubble it is likely that inflation is somehow being suppressed, allowing the excessive quantity of money relative to GDP to be sustained. If, as in the case of the US, the central bank maintains a loose policy and a comparatively high rate of money supply growth because inflation continues to remain suppressed, then the 'monetary excess' becomes even greater.

By 'monetary excess' we mean the supply of money relative to the demand to hold it. Normally, of course, supply and demand are brought into balance through a movement in price. The price of a country's money from the point of view of foreigners is the exchange rate for the currency, while the price of money from the point of view of domestic residents is the inverse of the general price level. That is, if prices of goods and services are higher, the 'price' – or value – of money is lower and conversely if the prices of goods and services are lower, the price of money is by definition higher. Therefore if the supply of money is exceeding the demand the price of money must fall, meaning that the general price level must rise, and the currency must fall in the foreign exchange markets. This is a more fundamental way of looking at the explanations of the monetary cycle advanced earlier in this chapter. If, as in the US economy from 1995–96 onwards, an apparent monetary excess is sustained (as observed, for example, in a high rate of money growth relative to GDP growth or a high level of liquidity indicators such as the example given) then these adjustments are not occurring and, in a sense, it appears wrong to suggest that there is a 'monetary excess'. If there is no price adjustment, in what sense can there be said to be an excess of supply (in this case, of money)?

The answer to this apparent paradox is that in a structural bubble the demand for money becomes, or is likely to become, part of the bubble as much as the demand for other assets. Because money is a substitute for the other financial assets, if they (that is shares and bonds) rise in price then money is also likely to rise in price (or value). This highlights the fact that a structural bubble is likely to require inflation of goods and services prices to remain suppressed. Otherwise the supply of money would have to be rising at an increasingly rapid rate. In the type of bubble where inflation remains suppressed a steady but high rate of money growth can be associated with rising, or high, prices of all financial assets including money. The external manifestation of the price of money is the exchange rate for the currency. In the present case of the US, this means the dollar remaining strong as long as the bubble sustains itself.

Insofar as the demand for money is strong during the structural bubble – along with the demand for other financial assets, and possibly some real assets also – then it might be argued that there is no 'monetary excess'. After all, the demand for money is strong, along with the supply, so in what way can there be said to be an excess? The problem with this argument is that it is analogous to the point of view taken by many investors and commentators during the internet mania, when they asked 'How can we say that these stocks are overvalued, given that the stock prices are those which equate supply and demand?' The answer is that most of the demand owes itself only to the existence of the bubble and will cease to be once the bubble is burst.

Could a structural bubble that raises the demand for money to meet the greater supply of money not last for ever, given that the stronger demand for money – which manifests in a strong currency – is associated with the suppression of inflation? Given that the structural bubble alters the structure of the economy, by definition, the 'fundamentals', or the yardsticks by which the valuations of assets are assessed, may change in a way that appears to justify the higher asset valuations of the bubble, in the manner of George Soros's 'Theory of Reflexivity'. The problem with this is that the bubble will inevitably exacerbate imbalances in the economy that are ultimately unsustainable. The imbalances that have been the product of the US financial bubble were discussed in the previous chapter, namely excessive debt, deficient savings and a growing external imbalance. The structural bubble encourages stronger domestic demand but it does not in itself encourage stronger demand overseas. The currency may be strengthened by capital inflow that is attracted by the bubble-boosted returns on investment but the deterioration in the balance of payments trade and current accounts is not sustainable indefinitely. Ultimately the net liabilities to foreigners will no longer be able to be financed at a high level for the currency. The currency, together with the demand for money as a whole, will fall into a decline that would be likely to turn into a collapse. At this point the accumulated monetary excess is effectively realized in a general inflation that will inevitably be attributed by observers to the devaluation of the currency.

Monetary Policy and Moral Hazard

The conclusion at this point is that if the US economy in late 2002 remains a bubble economy, then ultimately the dollar must decline severely in a collapse that will be inflationary in nature. But how can we really know that the US is a bubble economy, as opposed to an economy that is benefiting from improved productivity performance relative to the rest of the world and, as a result, attracting capital from the rest of the world? A little like a murder detective who would like to ascertain the suspect's motive as well as having the evidence, the economist should want to see that the circumstances conducive to a structural bubble were present, as well as seeing the evidence for the bubble. The evidence was discussed in the previous chapter, and very few people now dispute that the US experienced a stock market bubble at least in the late 1990s. For the circumstances, we return to the three conditions for a structural bubble suggested earlier in this chapter – initially permissive monetary policy with inflation remaining suppressed, a resilient or strong currency, and the support of the authorities.

Largely because inflation (so far) has remained low the argument is usually heard that monetary policies in the western world have been restrained, and that central banks have done an excellent job in keeping a lid on inflation, possibly even overdoing it in the manner of the Japanese authorities. However, money supply growth in the major western economies has certainly not been low, as discussed earlier, and if we look back to the early stages of the acceleration in stock markets – from the start of the bubble period in 1995–96 – those economists who do concern themselves with measures of monetary conditions already were warning that monetary policies were becoming unreasonably loose. This author wrote the following in early 1997 for *The LGT Guide to World Equity Markets 1997*, 'Very buoyant financial markets in 1996 and early 1997 reflected the accumulation of excessive liquidity in the world economy as central banks ... eased monetary policies further from the accommodative stances already established at the end of 1995.'[9] Morgan Stanley Dean Witter economist John Montgomery wrote in a March 1999 piece entitled *The Acceleration of Global Money Supplies:* 'They show an acceleration of global money supplies, in keeping with our view that global financial markets are awash in liquidity. A weighted average of broad money (M3 ...) accelerated from a 5.6 per cent rate of growth in 1996 (change from December 1995 to December 1996) to 6.6 per cent in 1997 and 7.3 per cent in 1998.'[10] Montgomery also showed that his global money supply estimate was growing significantly faster if deflationary Japan was excluded from the figures.

Through this period monetary policy was used as a means of supporting financial markets in times of crisis or uncertainty. The original easing of monetary policy in late 1995 was a reaction to an economic slowdown in 1995, that in turn was caused by excessive central bank tightening in 1994 and early 1995, particularly in Europe. In fact the whole easing of policy over 1995–96 can be seen as a central bank reaction to a prolonged period of excessively tight monetary policy during the first half of the decade, particularly in Europe where various central banks had been struggling to defend currency exchange rates. It was this prolonged period of monetary tightness that played a large part in cementing low inflation expectations across the globe, a mindset that was to persist into the current decade. However, from 1997 onwards financial market developments played an increasing role in influencing monetary policies. The Asian crisis of 1997–98 culminated in the Russian debt default and devaluation of August 1998 and the subsequent collapse of the highly leveraged hedge fund Long-Term Capital Management (LTCM) in October 1998. Reportedly LTCM was leveraged about 28 times, with assets of roughly US$130 billion resting on capital of only US$4.7 billion. The Fed's response was to cut interest rates three times in quick succession, an easing that was to provide the basis for the further acceleration in the ascent of the US stock market through 1999.

The maintenance of excessively loose policies in early 1999 was encouraged by a widespread (incorrect) view that the world economy was seriously threatened by the Asian and Russian shock. In 1998 and early 1999 the majority of economists believed that the world economy was at risk of serious weakness and that deflation was a major threat. The global economists at Crédit Suisse First Boston in London, for example, wrote in July 1998 in the introduction to a piece entitled 'Liquidity Please!': 'the 1999 output recovery ... is by no means assured: the significant and clearly asymmetric risk remains that of sliding into a more protracted world slump' (Crédit Suisse First Boston Fixed Income Research – Europe, 17 July 1998). By late 1998 the notion of a deflationary slump was conventional wisdom, and views about Europe, in particular, were extremely negative. Ed Hyman, the respected and very widely followed economic consultant, argued that deflation was almost inevitable in Europe in 1999, commenting, 'The UK may already be in recession, Germany, Europe's largest economy unfortunately is its weakest, Eastern European economies are in recessions, and Russia is in collapse' (ISI Group Economic Report, 16 February 1999). Samuel Brittan, writing in the *Financial Times*, echoed the general view of that newspaper at the time when he wrote, in late 1998, that the world faced a 'deeper than normal recession'.

It is probably unfair to single out individual views in this way because the opinions noted above were simply in line with conventional wisdom in early 1999 – that the world faced a deflationary slump. With this climate of opinion, it was not surprising that central banks felt very comfortable leaning on the side of extreme monetary laxity. But this view was completely wrong. The Asian and LTCM crises made barely a dent in the US economy, the growth of which continued to accelerate, driven on by loose money and the developing huge asset bubble. European economic activity, far from slumping, accelerated sharply from the spring of 1999 and the UK never came close to recession. Rather than falling into deflation, European inflation picked up during 1999 and remained continuously at or above the European Central Bank's acceptable limit of 2.0 per cent over the following years. The unwarranted further monetary easing in the US, echoed in Europe, had set the stage for the further acceleration of asset price inflation in 1999 and early 2000.

The Fed and the other western central banks did begin to raise interest rates during the second half of 1999. Beginning on 30 June 1999 the Fed raised rates six times, by a total of 1.75 per cent, over a period of 11 months, to reach a peak for the key federal funds rate of 6.5 per cent in May 2000. But with the economy booming and the stock market in the grip of speculative frenzy, a rate increase of this, comparatively modest, magnitude was not enough to reduce money supply growth. In fact the Fed deliberately kept the markets very well supplied with liquidity in late 1999 because by then it was concerned with another potentially disruptive influence – the millennium date change, or 'Y2K problem' as it was known. The concern was that older computer software and hardware and date-sensitive processors contained in all sorts of equipment would not be able to cope with the change to the year 2000 and might cease functioning completely, bringing about total chaos. Companies throughout the world spent billions of dollars ensuring systems were Y2K compliant and the investment banks and fund management companies expended substantial resources ensuring that the companies they invested in were safe from Y2K concerns. On the day, of course, nothing actually happened. A charitable view would be that the vast resources employed on the Y2K issue were successful in ensuring a smooth transition to the new millennium. A probably more accurate view would be that the hysteria about Y2K was in fact another manifestation of the technology frenzy, which carried with it the sense that the whole world was in thrall to the onward march of technology.

The initial Fed rate rises, in June, August and November 1999, elicited a sharply positive reaction from the US stock market, contrary to normal experience. By this time the market mania was at its most intense and all news was treated as good news. But the Fed helped to encourage the positive reaction by indicating that the rate rises would bring inflation under control, thereby hinting that no further rises were in store. With the August hike the Fed commented that the rate rises 'should markedly diminish the risk of rising inflation going forward'. For the stock market in its then state this amounted to raising a red rag to a bull. Following the November rate rise one widely followed US investment strategist commented, 'This means the Fed is out of our face until spring.' Given the rate at which the market indices, and more especially the favoured TMT stocks, were appreciating investors' time horizons could seemingly afford to be short and the Fed's soothing comments, in the ultra-loose liquidity environment, were enough to encourage the market to further sharp gains.

The tightening by foreign central banks was, if anything, more decisive than by the Fed, even though monetary conditions outside the US had been less lax than those within it. The fact that it was the Fed, again, that maintained a relatively looser policy was an important influence that allowed the US financial bubble to be perpetuated. The European Central Bank raised interest rates by 2.25 per cent over its tightening cycle, a slightly greater amount than the Fed, and was slower to reduce rates in 2001, only making its first cut in May 2001, more than four months after the US monetary authority.

By the time of the Fed's final rate increase in the sequence, which saw the federal funds rate increased by 0.5 per cent to 6.5 per cent on 16 May 2000, the stock market had already peaked, and the NASDAQ, in particular, had suffered a major, and very volatile, fall. Inevitably, many interested observers have blamed the Fed for raising rates too far and triggering the economic weakness that followed. Much vitriol was directed at Alan Greenspan from those who lost money in the NASDAQ crash. One of the perhaps slightly more considered criticisms, contained in a letter to a newspaper from a University of California professor, began as follows: 'The likely US recession may well end up being a product of the Federal Reserve's overly aggressive interest rate policy and, in part, of its underhanded attempt to deflate the technology stock "bubble" through six consecutive interest rate increases.' When a financial pyramid collapses, inevitably a cause of, or 'reason' for, the collapse is identified and those who have lost out will be quick to attribute blame. But when a giant house of cards collapses, how reasonable is it to blame the puff of wind or slight vibration of the ground that were the proximate cause? Greenspan's Fed was to blame, but for presiding over the building of the 'house of cards' in the first place, not for triggering the inevitable collapse.

The incredible acceleration of margin debt (that is loans by brokerages to investors collateralized by shares in their portfolios) in late 1999 and early 2000 was clear evidence of such a 'house of cards'. Margin debt is only a small part of consumer debt but its very direct relationship to stock market speculation makes it an important indicator of the degree of speculative euphoria. During 1999 the New York Stock Exchange measure of margin debt was setting successive new records both in absolute amount, having more than doubled since 1995, and relative to measures such as total personal income. By the end of 1999 and into the early months of 2000, margin debt accelerated sharply further, showing explosive monthly growth rates in excess of 10 per cent for some months.

In fact, contrary to the newspaper correspondent's claim, the Fed did not 'attempt to deflate the technology stock bubble' at all. Fed governors went out of their way not to do this, as shown by the way they attempted to soothe the markets' concerns with each rate rise. Earlier in 1999, in March, the Fed considered adopting a 'tightening bias', that is notifying the financial markets that a prospective increase in interest rates had become more likely, but at the time it did not do this partly because of fears it would unsettle the financial markets. The minutes of that meeting noted that a tightening bias 'would likely have ... a relatively pronounced and *undesired* effect on financial markets' (emphasis added).

The Fed's asymmetric approach to financial markets – stepping in with aggressive rate cuts when the stock market fell sharply but doing nothing, or even providing positive encouragement, when the market was appreciating exponentially – was part of a pattern of the Greenspan Fed that constituted what came to be known as the 'Greenspan put'. The 'put' refers to a put option – a financial contract that gives the owner the right to sell a specified financial asset some time in the future at a price agreed as part of the contract. The idea is that investors in the US stock market had a virtually guaranteed exit from the market if required, similar to holding a put option, because they could be certain that the Fed would underwrite the market in the event of a serious decline. This creates 'moral hazard', the much-discussed phenomenon whereby investors undertake excessively risky investments in the belief that they are protected from losses.

In retrospect, the creation of moral hazard in the US stock market goes right back to the very early days of the Greenspan Fed, when the Fed stepped in with aggressive interest rate cuts following the stock market crash of 19 October 1987. At the time the Fed was universally praised for its action in the wake of what was an unprecedented market collapse, greater even than the crash of 1929, which could potentially have done untold damage to the financial system and the economy. However, a pattern of market intervention was set. Logically, it might have been thought that risk premiums on equities (that is the degree of risk priced into equities by investors, discussed in the following chapter) might have risen after the 1987 crash, given the unprecedented volatility that the stock markets displayed. However, it was not long before risk premiums were on their downtrend to record lows – and valuations of equities to corresponding record highs. It seems that the lesson that investors drew from the 1987 crash was not that equities were more risky than had previously been believed but that they were more secure, given that the Fed could be relied upon to step in, in the event of trouble.

This message was reinforced by the later Fed actions, including the response to the LTCM crisis. Alan Greenspan's argument at the time of the LTCM crisis monetary loosening was that Fed interest rate cuts were not aimed at supporting the stock market, but rather providing liquidity to the corporate debt markets, which had appeared to be seizing up as the yield spreads relative to US Treasury bonds widened sharply. But this argument was disingenuous at best. As discussed in the following chapter, financial markets cannot be viewed in isolation. They are all priced relative to each other and simultaneously off the liquidity and risk environment. Action cannot be taken to support one financial market without having immediate implications for the other markets. Furthermore, as was discussed in the previous chapter, the widening of credit spreads can now be seen as a trend that went beyond the LTCM crisis, and in a more fundamental way was a symptom of the stresses on the US financial system imposed by the growing economic imbalances that were themselves a function of the financial bubble. By cutting interest rates and injecting more liquidity into the economy, the Fed was responding to a problem that had its origins in excessively loose monetary policy by loosening even further.

The Fed's direct contribution to the moral hazard that played an important part in the building of the giant financial bubble has been well recognized. Less well understood is the way that the Fed's action has been part of a much wider picture that has led investors to have an unjustified faith in the power of governments and central banks, that represents a complete reversal of previous attitudes. Stephen Roach, Morgan Stanley Dean Witter's perceptive global economist, put it thus in June 1999:

'Policy makers are in charge as never before. World financial markets are being increasingly dominated by the spin and action of those officials empowered to set monetary, fiscal, currency, and regulatory policies. There is a certain irony to this development. For a world rushing to embrace market-based capitalism, this concentration of power in the hands of the policy-making elite adds a new tension to financial markets. It is more important than ever to get policy right.'[11]

It was not always like this. Even as recently as the early 1990s, investors tended to distrust the efficacy of central bank and government policy and by instinct often tended to go in the opposite direction to the one that policy was trying to push them. For instance, if a central bank intervened to support a currency, the trader's instinct was to sell it on the grounds that intervention in opposition to market forces would ultimately inevitably fail. By the end of the decade, a new generation of investors and traders saw things completely differently, and their instinct would be to buy a (major) currency if a central bank was intervening in its favour. This change in attitudes represented another change in perceived orthodoxy brought about by the bubble period that was both a function of the bubble and a contributor to it.

The key point here is that during the 1990s central banks more and more allowed their policy direction to be led by the financial markets, responding to signals from the financial markets as well as concerns in the markets. Increasingly, therefore, they were 'on the same side as the markets' rather than acting as 'referees'. Many would undoubtedly see this as a good thing, but the failure of the central banks to act neutrally with respect to the financial markets potentially creates all manner of 'feedback effects' once a financial bubble is developing. For instance, if central bank policy is set according to consensus market opinion then it creates a very strong incentive for all analysts, economists and so on to agree with consensus opinion, thereby strengthening the consensus and making the central bank more likely to take note. So, for example, if there is a consensus view in the markets that the failure of the central bank to cut interest rates would likely cause a recession, then it pays all market participants to agree with that view because if the central bank follows the consensus they cannot be wrong (in appearance at least). The central bank, following the consensus, cuts interest rates, citing the risk of recession if it does not do so, a move applauded by the markets. If there is no recession the market participants claim that recession was avoided because the central bank cut rates. If there is a recession market participants highlight how right they were to warn of the risk of recession, and 'what a shame that the central bank did not cut rates more'. This example, in fact, pretty much describes the situation at the end of 1998. The markets and the central banks end up 'on the same side'.

There is more to moral hazard even than central bank interest rate policy, considered broadly. The exhortations of government officials to invest in stocks, exampled in the previous chapter, and interventions in the currency markets and also in the gold market all played a part in increasing investors' feelings of security with equities, while at the same time undermining alternative asset classes. Gold is discussed in particular in Chapter 5. It tends to be dismissed by most investors as an 'ancient relic' of no real value, but in reality it is the only clear alternative to fiat monies (that is paper money) considered as a whole. At a time when the central banks of the major western economies were all pursuing highly expansionary monetary policies, gold should have been a natural investment alternative to money (that is bank deposits). But central banks' collective actions in aggressively selling gold from reserves to increase their investments in financial markets in the late 1990s, served to reinforce the message that financial instruments were better investments than gold. This boosted the demand for money at the expense of gold, while at the same time, in depressing the price of gold, contributed artificially to lowering inflation expectations, for which gold still serves as one of the indicators.

Interventions in the foreign exchange markets were also important. In this chapter it has been emphasized that the strong (and heavily overvalued) dollar has been absolutely integral to the US structural bubble, both as a cause and effect, that is a key component of the 'feedback loops' that characterize all asset bubbles. Seen in this light, heavy central bank interventions in favour of the dollar have played a major role in sustaining the US bubble economy. Not all central bank foreign exchange intervention in recent years has been dollar supportive. The European Central Bank has intervened to support the euro. However, by far the bulk of overall central bank activity in foreign exchange has been in favour of the dollar, particularly that by the Bank of Japan (BOJ), as it has repeatedly tried to resist yen appreciation. Estimates place Bank of Japan intervention to prevent the yen rising from May to September 1999 at nearly US$50 billion, and a further US$25 billion was estimated to have been purchased in interventions during the autumn of 2001. When taken together with heavy continuous purchases of dollars by other Asian central banks, this amounts to a significant element of the net capital inflow to the US that has financed the current account deficit at a high exchange rate for the dollar, and sustained the financial bubble.

It is also worthwhile mentioning the large investment banks, which have increasingly been seen to act together at times of financial crisis. The LTCM crisis was resolved as a result of the New York Fed bringing together 14 banks and securities houses to arrange the takeover of LTCM. The concern at the time was that if LTCM was forced to unwind its huge positions all at once there could be cataclysmic consequences for the various markets in which it was involved. Given what we now know, however, it is reasonable to ask whether it might not have been better to let whatever might have happened happen, rather than effectively bailing out those who were taking increasingly risky bets on the existing market trends continuing. By arranging the bailout the New York Fed and the investment banks again gave the green light for investors to continue to buy growth stocks, to continue to sell gold, to continue to buy the dollar and generally to go with the trends that had been working, then backed up by an additional shot of liquidity following the Fed's accompanying monetary ease. So was the bubble made even larger.

Following the September 11th tragedy, with the equities markets by then in a steep downtrend, the banks again got together with the aim of protecting markets in the wake of the closure of the New York Stock Exchange by discouraging 'unnecessary' foreign exchange trading and short-selling in equities. The US Securities and Exchange Commission also eased various regulations to make it easier for companies to repurchase shares and for mutual funds to borrow funds to meet any redemptions.

All of these actions considered individually – the behaviour of the investment banks following September 11th, the BOJ's efforts to prevent the yen appreciating, the Fed cutting interest rates at times of financial stress and so on – are very understandable, often laudable considered in isolation. However, together they add up to a pattern that sends a signal to investors that the full weight of all possible powers will be brought to bear to protect the downside in financial markets at times of severe stress. The fact that all the actions of the authorities that have been discussed work in the same direction – that is to increase the demand for financial assets, and dollar financial assets in particular – is not because there is some sort of conspiracy but because the authorities, and central banks in particular, have become hostage to the financial market monster they have helped to create. It is logical to believe that the death of this monster must also be associated with the death of the process that helped to create it. This means in the end a reversion to the healthy scepticism that existed towards central banks and their policies in the 1980s, and a collapse of confidence in the value of the 'Greenspan put'. At the end of 2002 we may be some way towards this, but there is clearly a long way to go. The disturbing implications are discussed in the final chapter of this book.

In summary, loose monetary policy, the persistence of low inflation, and the authorities' encouragement to investors as well as their willingness to use monetary policy and other measures to support financial markets in the event of problems, all suggest an environment that was highly conducive to the formation of a structural bubble in the US, and to some extent in the rest of the western world, from 1995–96 onwards. As discussed in the previous chapter, and as is now widely recognized, the extremes witnessed in stock markets in 1999 and 2000 constituted a bubble of a magnitude unprecedented in history. Given that high measured productivity growth can be a function of a bubble environment, as was also discussed in the previous chapter, it surely makes sense to ignore the message from productivity growth until after the bubble has fully unwound, rather than, as some economists have been inclined to do, build an analysis of the US economy upon a presumption of sustained high productivity growth. Like the murder detective with the suspect, the motive and the evidence, with the evidence of a giant bubble and the circumstances for its creation it makes sense for the analyst to assume that there is a structural bubble and explain any other phenomena observed within that context.

In this chapter it has been explained that, logically, the full unwinding of a structural bubble against a background of loose monetary conditions sustained by aggressive central bank action must involve severe currency weakness and ultimately inflation. Until this has occurred the structural bubble has not fully unwound. Even though equity prices may have collapsed, the bubble may simply have emerged in other markets such as bonds, or perhaps real estate. In the next chapter this is explored further through consideration of the relationship between the valuation of equity and bond markets.

CHAPTER 4

The Reversion to Long-term Value

The Valuation of Stock and Bond Markets

The liquidity indicators illustrated in the previous chapter showed that loose monetary policy was a key element – a necessary although not sufficient condition – for the building of the giant financial bubble that was the dominating influence over the US economy, and the global economy, by the year 2000. They also showed that the tightening of monetary policy over 1999–2000, while enough to tip by then unstable stock markets into a prolonged and severe bear market, by historic standards was not particularly major. It was more of a (temporary) return from an extremely loose policy towards a neutral policy, rather than a move to tight monetary conditions in an absolute sense. Once the financial bubble began to unwind, though, even a Fed monetary policy easing of unprecedented aggressiveness could not prevent the slide in stock prices. Many stock market analysts, used to the idea that a series of Fed rate cuts 'always' presages a new bull market, argued early in 2001 that investors should not 'fight the Fed'. But for once Fed policy proved to be impotent, at least with respect to the stock market. The years 2000–01 marked not merely a cyclical turning point but also a secular turning point to a new financial era during which the structure of the financial bubble will be dismantled and many of the beliefs that characterized the bubble period – including investors' total faith in central banks and central bankers – will be overturned.

Professional investment strategists conventionally focus on measures of liquidity, profits (or earnings) growth and measures of valuation to determine whether or not a particular stock market represents a potentially good investment and to help determine the allocation of assets between equity markets. Liquidity is often given the highest weight when the investment decision is for a reasonably short time horizon (less than a year or so). The financial history of the post-war period supports the case for stressing liquidity factors as the dominant influence over the equity market cycle, as borne out for the last 20 years by the global liquidity indicator charted in the previous chapter. However, clearly during the present unwinding of the structural bubble liquidity has lost its potency as a determinant of financial market behaviour. The lesson is that even generous injections of liquidity into the economy cannot rebuild a pyramid once it has begun to collapse.

The idea that liquidity is not being a helpful indicator leads naturally to the thought that measures of valuation might be useful in determining a bottom to the equity market. After all, the equity market peak was marked by extremes in most commonly used measures of valuation. The problem is that most common measures of valuation are anchored in concepts (such as current corporate earnings) that are not independent of the building and bursting of the bubble. This has already been touched upon, and will be explored further in Chapter 6. During the bubble era, companies were able to boost earnings per share by increasing leverage, making acquisitions, investing in other companies, benefiting from appreciation of their pension funds, selling equipment and services to start-up companies, earning fees from the inflated levels of stock markets and the inflated level of merger and acquisition activity (in the case of the investment banks) and so on. This all served to boost corporate earnings until the bubble burst, when earnings were simultaneously deflated. So using a measure of stock market valuation that incorporates corporate earnings as a benchmark (for example the price–earnings ratio) is not necessarily going to be a useful indicator for a stock market bottom. The valuation measure may suggest, based on historical experience, a market bottom, but then a further decline in equities prices could undermine the valuation benchmark (for example the measures of corporate earnings).

The types of valuation measures that asset allocators use are even less useful in a financial bubble. These are measures that in various ways compare the yields on stocks with the yield on long-term government bonds. A common such indicator is the bond yield–earnings yield ratio. The earnings yield on the stock market is 100 divided by the price–earnings ratio for the market, that is the earnings for the index expressed as a percentage of the index. If the ratio of (or the difference between) the bond yield and the earnings yield is high relative to its historic range then the market is judged to be 'overvalued' (earnings yields are 'too low') and if it is low relative to its history the market is considered to be 'undervalued'.

The earnings yield ratio (or the similar dividend yield ratio) is a poor measure of valuation for a reason that is well known, which is that inflation affects stock earnings yields and bond yields differently. A bond yield incorporates an expectation for annualized inflation over the life of the bond because the bond's coupon is fixed in money terms and the investor in bonds will therefore require to be compensated for higher prospective inflation with a higher yield. Stock earnings yields (or dividend yields) are in theory (not empirically) independent of inflation because the investor is compensated if future inflation is high since stock dividends and earnings should rise along with price levels in the economy. Both the earnings (the numerator in the earnings yield calculation) and the stock price (the denominator) should, over a long period of time, move roughly in a way that reflects price levels, meaning that the ratio of the two is independent of inflation.

So, for example in an extreme case, if inflation is becoming completely out of control and is widely expected to average 50 per cent annually over the next 10 years, the 10-year government bond yield would need to be well over 50 per cent (to provide investors with a real return) but the stock dividend or earnings yields would not be anything like this level. Investors in stocks are inflation-proofed, at least to some extent, by the fact that corporate profits will be rising rapidly in money terms with the high levels of inflation. Investors in conventional long-term bonds, with a fixed coupon, do not have this inflation protection, other than that which is built into the yield. In this example, therefore, the ratio of the bond yield to stock yields would be very high, and completely out of line with historic experience assuming, in the past, inflation had been well under control. Then, a very high level of the bond yield–earnings yield ratio would not necessarily be a sign that stocks are expensive, but merely an indicator of a high expected inflation rate.

During the big bubble, inflation (at least as measured by official consumer price inflation data) remained low and fairly stable. Therefore the drawback of the bond yield–earnings yield ratio, of not being independent of inflation, was not so important. There was a much bigger, less well-understood problem that meant that yield ratio type measures failed to pick up the massive extent of the overvaluation of stock markets at the top of the bubble, and have tended to make stock markets appear fairly valued or undervalued through the subsequent long bear market. This is that equity yields and bond yields are not independent of each other, and in a bubble environment low equity yields can lead to low bond yields just as much as low bond yields can produce low equity yields. The argument here has already been made with respect to money (bank deposits) in the previous chapter. This is that all financial assets are substitutes for each other to some degree. The managers of the large investment funds, after all, actively allocate funds between equities, bonds and cash. In a liquidity-powered bubble, as equities are driven higher and higher there is likely to be some reallocation towards bonds, and then cash, increasing the demand for these financial assets also. In a giant financial bubble such as that from 1995–2000 the demand for all financial assets increases, including, as discussed in the last chapter, money. The demand for bonds will increase and yields will be pushed down. Comparing yields on stocks and yields on bonds is not much better, as an approach to valuation, than comparing valuations of different internet stocks. Yield ratios are merely a measure of relative valuation and do not necessarily tell the investor anything about absolute value.

A good measure of equities' absolute value has to be anchored in a measure of corporate worth that is largely independent of the financial markets. One such measure, that is championed in particular by London-based financial consultant Andrew Smithers, is Tobin's Q, the ratio of market capitalization to the replacement cost of corporate net assets (see Andrew Smithers and Stephen Wright *Valuing Wall Street*).[12] This ratio directly compares the values that the financial markets are placing on companies with the actual value of the physical assets they own. In theory, if the ratio is more than one (that is the market is valuing companies at more than the worth of their net assets) then the market is expensive and companies, on average, would be well advised to undertake new real investment rather than acquire other companies. If the ratio is less than one then the market is cheap, and the reverse applies.

The many criticisms of Tobin's Q as a market valuation tool are unfounded. A common criticism is that corporate net assets do not include the human, or intellectual, capital that comprises many of the corporations of today's 'weightless economy'. This criticism is wrong because the employees of, for instance, the investment banks or the computer software companies are not actually 'owned' by the companies and therefore their shareholders. The return on their human capital accrues to the employees themselves and, in a free market, they are able to take their skills and experience elsewhere. Nevertheless, Tobin's Q does require for its calculation data that may not always be available for all markets on a timely basis, and even where data is available – for the US for instance – there may be reasons to doubt its accuracy.

As already mentioned, price earnings ratios for stock markets on their own are not a good measure of valuation in a structural bubble because the earnings for the stock market become dependent on the bubble, that is the earnings are not independent of the price. One way of overcoming, or diminishing the extent of, this problem is to consider a price–earnings ratio in the form of the ratio of the index level to a rolling average of earnings for the index over a very long period, for example a 10-year average of earnings. Assuming the rolling average is calculated over a long enough period, this helps to overcome the problem that the earnings for the stock market could be bubble-inflated, because the bubble-inflated years will only form a proportion of the years that are being averaged, thereby diluting their influence on the total measure. On the other hand, this measure implicitly ignores the possibility that there could be genuine change that has accelerated earnings

growth. This way of looking at price–earnings ratios was proposed as long
as 70 years ago by Graham and Dodd in their classic book on security analysis[13] and, much more recently and in other variations, by Robert Shiller. On
this basis the S&P 500 index of the US equity market attained a completely
unprecedented ratio of over 45 at the market peaks. At the previous highs
in 1929, this 10-year P/E ratio for the US market reached a much lower
multiple, between 30 and 35.

A relationship between stock dividend yields and bond yields falls out of
the well-known identity that derives from the 'Gordon growth model'. If
dividends per share maintain a constant growth rate then the equity investor
receives a total annualized return from equities equal to the dividend yield
plus this growth rate of dividends. In this simple model it can be shown
fairly easily that the stock market will appreciate at the rate of growth of
dividends per share, meaning that this growth rate will be the capital gain
part of the return that accrues to the investor. The return that investors expect
from their investment can be expressed as the risk-free rate plus the additional return they expect to receive to compensate them for taking on the
greater volatility associated with equity markets. In equilibrium, this expected return and the actual return should be the same, meaning that the risk-
free rate plus the risk premium (that is the element of the return required to
compensate for the riskiness of the investment) must equal the dividend
yield plus the growth rate of dividends. This means that the appropriate dividend yield can be expressed as the risk-free rate plus the risk premium
minus the dividend growth rate, simply by rearranging the expression. The
dividend yield is the dividend divided by the price and this therefore produces a valuation identity for the level of the stock market.

In equilibrium the cost of capital and the return on capital should be equal.
Investors' expected return – the risk-free rate plus the risk premium – is the
cost of capital for companies, at which their future earnings and dividend
stream are being discounted. The risk-free rate is usually understood to be
the yield on long-term government bonds because these are effectively free
of bankruptcy risk. If we consider the identity in nominal terms (that is not
adjusted for inflation) it confirms the inappropriateness of comparing
directly dividend yields (or earnings yields) and bond yields. In equilibrium
the dividend yield is equal to the bond yield plus the risk premium minus
the dividend growth rate (from before, where the risk-free rate is taken to
be the bond yield). Rearranging, the bond yield minus the dividend yield
will therefore be equal to the dividend growth rate minus the risk premium.
In theory there is no tendency for this difference to be stable on average
over time (in statistical jargon it is not mean reverting) because the dividend
growth rate incorporates inflation that could be any number indefinitely.
This shows that the spread between the bond yield and the dividend yield

(or the earnings yield) cannot be used as a stable basis for valuing the equities market, although in a period of fairly steady inflation it could appear to work reasonably.

However, it has already been noted that there is a more fundamental flaw in the common approaches to valuation than the fact that yield ratio (or yield gap) measures are not theoretically mean reverting. It is that bond yields are not an appropriate benchmark to use in valuing equities, at least in the midst of a structural financial bubble. The problem is that although the yield on long-term government bonds is invariably treated as the risk-free rate, long-term government bonds are not risk-free investments. The investors' capital is only secured in nominal terms (in conventional bonds) and bond markets are highly volatile over shorter-term periods, which means that the investor is at risk of, possibly substantial, capital losses unless he is prepared to hold the bond investment for many years. A genuine risk-free return, annualized over a long period, can only be achieved theoretically, not by holding government debt (although a case could be made for inflation indexed bonds), but by holding an extremely diversified portfolio of investments in the equity of the world economy; so diversified, in fact, that it contains a stake in all of the productive assets of the (open) world economy (that is the majority of the world economy that is open to foreign investment). By definition, there can then be no risk (or at least risk is reduced to the minimum possible) because the investor has a stake in everything that is able to produce a return in the entire world.

This may be fine in theory, but it is clearly impossible in practice, so how can we know what this hypothetical risk-free rate is? In fact, it is fairly easy to estimate it roughly in real (that is inflation-adjusted) terms because over time it must equate to the trend real growth rate of the (open) world economy. In a steady state in which all the growth rates remain constant, the growth of the productive assets of the world economy would be equal to the economic growth rate. The earnings yield on these assets represents incomes that can be reinvested to sustain the growth rate, and in equilibrium this yield will equate to the growth rate. This yield represents the total return that the hypothetical investor in all of the world's productive assets would receive and therefore it is the risk-free return. In short, the risk-free return should be equal to the trend real growth rate of the global economy.

This suggests that over time government bonds should not yield less than the trend economic growth rate in real terms, and probably should yield somewhat more given that they are not entirely free of risk from the point of view of the investor. Between 1972 and 2000 the OECD (that is the developed) countries as a whole displayed a trend growth rate of 2.8 per cent per annum, obviously with substantial cycles around this trend. If this were to remain the trend growth rate it implies that long-term government bonds would be unable to yield less than 2.8 per cent in real terms on a sustained basis. In practice, 3.0–3.5 per cent has often been seen as a reasonable real return expectation for investors in long-term government bonds.

If we consider world equities as a whole, and we bear in mind the hypothetical investor able to invest in all of the world's assets, we can consider the earnings yield on the global equity market as approximating to the investor's total annualized real return. The return will be made up in practice of dividends, and capital growth that will equate to the growth rate of the dividends over time. But if the total of the world market's earnings were paid out as a dividend, then there would be no dividend *per share* growth, in theory. The dividends would have to be reinvested in new equity to sustain the growth rate, meaning that the number of new shares would grow at the same rate as total dividends and there would be no growth in dividends per share. In this case the investor's total return would be the dividend yield, which would be the same as the earnings yield. The opposite extreme would occur if the companies that make up the world market paid virtually no dividends to investors. The dividend yield would be nearly nothing but the earnings would be available for reinvestment, producing the growth from which the investor benefits in the form of capital gain. In the positions between these two extremes the investor receives both a dividend yield and a real capital gain that equates to the growth of dividends per share over time. In theory it is reasonable to assume that these two elements of the total return will add up to the earnings yield on the world market.

In a totally 'riskless' world therefore, we can hypothesize that a 'steady state' would occur if the real interest rate and the earnings yield on the global equity market were both equal and equal to the long-run annual growth rate of the world economy. Over the past 30 years this growth rate, at least for the developed world, has been 2.8 per cent. This sets a sort of theoretical lower bound on the prospective earnings yield for the world market – at least based on this backward-looking growth rate – of 2.8 per cent. The price–earnings (P/E) ratio is the inverse of the earnings yield (or 100 divided by the yield when the yield is expressed as a percentage), meaning that a 2.8 per cent yield equates to a theoretical maximum price–earnings ratio for the world market of around 35.

In practice, of course, this 'theoretical maximum P/E' is meaningless because financial assets are not 'riskless' from the point of view of any investor. As already suggested, government bonds should probably not be considered an entirely risk-free investment and equities are clearly not. To estimate a rough fair P/E ratio for the world equity market over the long-term we need to know what is an appropriate compensation for risk (that is equity risk premium) that needs to be added in to arrive at a fair earnings yield. There have been countless studies aimed at establishing fair equity risk premiums for various stock markets. The most obvious way to approach the question is simply to look at the long-term historic returns, because this tells us the return to risk that investors have actually received in the past. Unfortunately there are three major potential problems with using historic data for market returns to estimate an appropriate current risk premium: first, depending on the historic period chosen, it is not obviously the case that the actual real returns received by investors were in line with the returns that investors had expected to receive, even if the period is a very long one. It is the expected future returns that are the key to the valuation of the stock market at any one time; second, the numbers for historic returns are surprisingly sensitive to the start and end date chosen for the estimate of annualized returns, although this problem can be overcome by fitting a long-run trend to equity market performance; third, it is not clear that the historically derived number will be appropriate for today's markets. For instance, equity investment may have become less risky if there are now more opportunities for diversification or if the management of economies has substantially improved.

The possibility that the 'fair' level for the equity risk premium had fallen was used to justify the valuation levels that stock markets had reached by 1999–2000 in some of the more considered analyses of the time. As Figure 4.1 (using data from the database of Thomson Financial Datastream) shows, the world market as a whole was trading on a P/E ratio of over 30 at its 2000 peak. The US stock market alone, based on the S&P 500 index, reached a P/E ratio calculated on trailing earnings of 36 at the top of the market. As earnings slumped in 2001 the P/E ratio on this basis soared even higher, reaching a high of 47, far in excess of any valuation peak ever seen before in 130 years of recorded financial history. These are valuation levels that leave very little, if any, prospective excess return in equities to compensate the investor for risk.

Figure 4.1 World market P/E ratio

The fact that we now know that these market peaks represented a bubble, and that markets have fallen so severely, rather undermines the argument – which was always dubious at best – that the developments in the world economy and financial system had been such as to make equity investment much less risky than it had been in the recent past. For the US market alone the marked increase in indebtedness and financial leverage of the corporate sector, as US companies borrowed to fund massive share buy-backs, in fact argued in the opposite direction. According to one estimate the debt to equity ratio of the S&P 500 companies in aggregate had risen to 116 per cent roughly by the time of the equity market peak, higher than the 84 per cent level at the end of the junk bond boom in 1990. On the assumption that the US economy was going to be growing more rapidly than the rest of the developed world – the standard assumption at the time – greater financial leverage could have made sense in terms of boosting the return on equity. However, the lower equity base, relatively, should have in theory demanded a higher equity risk premium to compensate for the greater financial risk in equities.

On the other hand, the old historic notion of an appropriate equity risk premium as high as 6 per cent is also almost certainly wrong. The 6 per cent figure was derived from past excess returns on equities over government bonds, but the historic real returns on bonds were artificially depressed by unanticipated high inflation. The more respectable studies have placed the appropriate long-run equity risk premium in the range 3–4 per cent. This is indeed exactly in accordance with the long-run trend in real total returns from US and UK equities – if we ignore the bubble period of the 1990s – assuming that the risk-free return is 3 per cent or a little over, as discussed above. A trend line fitted to UK equity real returns suggests a long-run annualized total real return of 6.5 per cent, while large company stocks in the US provided a total annualized real return to investors of 6.7 per cent over 1925–90. These numbers are roughly consistent with a risk premium for equities of 3.5 per cent, given an assumed risk-free return of 3 per cent. As an aside, it is interesting to note, though, that if the US numbers are taken to close to the end of the bubble period in 1999, rather than to 1990, the annualized total real return on US equities from 1925 rises to 8.0 per cent, illustrating the sensitivity of the result to the start and end point chosen for the calculation.

For the world as a whole, as previously explained, it can be assumed that the expected total real return from equities will, over time, approximate to the earnings yield, as the earnings yield is the ultimate source of the return. The P/E ratio is the inverse of the earnings yield. A 'fair' earnings yield of 6.5 per cent – based on an equity risk premium of 3.5 per cent – would equate to a P/E ratio of 15–16, roughly in line with long-run average

P/E ratios for the US and UK stock markets. Late in 2002 the major markets are still trading on P/E ratios significantly higher than this.

The Overvaluation of Bonds

Figure 4.2 compares the earnings yield on the world equity market (Thomson Financial Datastream data) with the measure of the global real interest rate (based on 10-year government bond yields for the major economies) that was introduced in Chapter 2. The difference between the two lines on the chart can be interpreted as a measure of the observed equity risk premium, that is it represents the prospective excess return on equities relative to bonds. As can be seen, this observed equity risk premium has fluctuated very widely over the past 30 years, having been in excess of 10 per cent through much of the 1970s, but disappearing to nothing around the time of the 1987 stock market crash and the 2000 equity market peak. A common interpretation would be to argue that equity markets were extremely cheap in the 1970s but had become very expensive by the time of the 1987 crash and the 1999–2000 market peak.

However, the chart shows up that this would be only a partial story because, in common with most stock market strategists, in making this observation we are basing our assessment of the valuation of equity markets upon the market-determined values of bonds. The implicit assumption in much valuation work is that the market correctly values government bonds at all times and it is reasonable to base the assessment of the fair value level of equities upon this market-determined level of bond yields. In fact the chart, in which the global real interest rate is calculated directly from bond

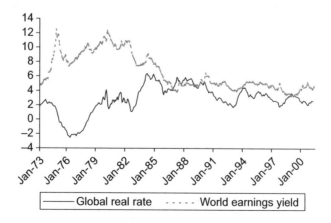

Figure 4.2 World earnings yield and real interest rate

yields in the market, suggests that this approach is misleading at best. As already suggested, the global real interest rate should tend to revert to a level of at least 3 per cent, but it has been far below this (in the 1970s) and far above 3 per cent (in the 1980s). Bond markets underestimated the 1970s inflation and were too conservative with regard to the potential for 'disinflation' in the 1980s and 1990s. Bonds were overvalued in the 1970s and undervalued during much of the 1980s.

At face value the equity risk premium derived from the chart above makes it look as if equities were very overvalued in 2000, but not actually more so than in 1987, when this measured equity risk premium also fell negative. This is the sort of conclusion that many stock market strategists, who compare equity yields and bond yields, have reached. This conclusion holds out the hope that by late in 2002 the valuation excesses in equities would have been mostly washed out and normality, promising decent equity returns in future, could soon be restored. The conclusion is wrong because it ignores the fact that at the end of 2002, and following a 22-year secular bull market, government bonds are grossly overvalued. In September 1987 the estimate of the global real interest rate shown in the chart above stood at nearly 6 per cent, implying bonds were undervalued from a very long-term perspective. By the end of 2002, this measure had fallen well below 2 per cent, implying that bonds are overvalued even if we assume that the very low inflation expectations built into markets prove to be justified. It will be argued below that the overvaluation of government bonds is even greater than this real interest rate measure implies. So, what the data actually show is that equity markets are still somewhat expensive relative to government bond markets that are themselves very overvalued.

A chart included in Chapter 2 (Figure 2.4) compared the global real interest rate measure above with the annual growth rate of industrial production for the OECD countries for the period 1980–2001. This chart provided evidence that the overvaluation of global bond markets began to emerge from the mid-1990s, coinciding with the development of the stock market bubble. It was from this time until the stock market peak that the global real interest rate began to look increasingly too low relative to production growth, compared with the previous history. It was suggested in Chapter 2 that this fall in the real interest rate below previous norms must have been either the result of a decline in prospective trend economic growth for the OECD or an excess of liquidity in the world economy, or both. The idea that the trend in economic growth rate for the developed economies might be declining stood in direct contradiction to the notion in financial markets at the time, which was that the trend economic growth rate had increased because of the advances in technology and communications.

The clear overvaluation of bonds that tended to become progressively greater from 1995 (after there had been a bond market 'crash' in 1994) was a natural consequence of the bubble that was developing in the equity markets. Figure 4.3 shows the ratio of the total return index for US stocks to the total return index for the 10-year US Treasury bond (data from Thomson Financial Datastream). This is expressed in logarithmic form, so that a constant rate of out-performance of equities relative to bonds over time will show as a steady rise in the line on the graph rather than as the exponentially rising line that would appear if the actual data, rather than logs, were plotted. The chart shows that there was a fairly steady trend of out-performance of stocks relative to bonds from 1980 until about 1995, from which time stocks' out-performance accelerated sharply until the peak of the stock market in March 2000. Since the stock market peak it is government bonds that have been out-performing sharply and during 2002 the relative return shown in the chart has dropped back to the upward-sloping line that represented the pre-1995 trend.

It might be tempting to think that the acceleration in the rate of stock market appreciation as the bubble intensified from 1995–96 would naturally have been bad for bonds, as money flows would have been increasingly directed towards stocks. This would be to misunderstand the nature of the development of the financial bubble, at least in its early stages. As already mentioned, the different classes of financial asset are first and foremost substitutes for each other. Corporate bonds are a reasonable substitute for equity, and government bonds are a partial substitute for corporate bonds. Cash could be a partial substitute for government bonds. In the earlier, liquidity-driven, stages of the bubble it is likely that if one financial asset class (equities) is being driven up to increasingly overvalued levels, then other, close substitute, asset classes will be pulled up also unless afflicted by specific problems. In the case of government bonds this is made even more

Figure 4.3 US total return on stocks relative to 10-year bond in log form

likely by the fact that the professional investors running the large bond and equity 'balanced' funds are making investment decisions that hinge explicitly on the relative valuation of the two asset classes. It is true that in the advanced stages of mania (which in the 1990s bubble might be judged to have been entered by 1998), when the frenzy has taken on a life of its own almost independent of the provision of liquidity to the economy, that the accelerating appreciation of the financial assets which best represent investors' justification for the mania (the 'TMT' stocks over 1998–2000) can start to be at the expense of the other asset classes and other areas of the economy. This is when the bubble does the most economic harm, and was discussed in Chapter 2.

In the case of bonds, the US and other government bond markets did suffer in 1999 as the internet boom entered its most frenzied phase and the Fed began to raise interest rates. However, until then they gave investors a total rate of return that was completely consistent with the very high trend rate that they had returned since the 1980s, an annualized rate of return of about 9 per cent since 1986 (it was even higher in the early part of the bond secular bull market). Given that the major improvement in inflation had already occurred by the mid-1990s, the continuation of these sorts of rates of return until 1999 provides circumstantial evidence that the bubble in equities spread into a bubble in bonds from 1995 onwards, as common sense would suggest likely.

As the equity bubble imploded from 2000, bonds appreciated again, even more rapidly, as investors did then switch out of equities and into bonds, pushing yields on 10-year US Treasury bonds to 40-year lows. The bear move in bonds in 1999 was not that substantial relative to the bull years that had preceded it and if, as argued here, the performance of bonds from 1995 was in the nature of a bubble then 1999 was only a 'correction' phase in this bubble (similar to late 1998 in the equity market), not part of the bursting of it. In short, the developing mania in equity markets pulled bonds up with it from 1995, but then bonds benefited even further as the equity market pyramid unravelled, pushing long-term government bonds to even more extremely overvalued levels. This was only possible because of the aggressively loose monetary policies implemented by the central banks, and the Fed in particular, from early 2001.

Economist Peter Warburton, in his book *Debt and Delusion*,[14] points out that a complete collapse of western equity markets is unlikely as long as bonds are performing strongly. A key theme of his book is that the incredible strength of bond markets over more than 20 years has become increasingly inconsistent with fundamental developments, in particular the weakening trend in national saving rates and the need for the market to absorb an increasing supply of new bond issues. Warburton argues that central banks have effectively underwritten yield curve arbitrage, allowing large investors and hedge funds to make money virtually risklessly by borrowing short term to fund positions in long-term debt. The central banks have done this by being prepared to keep short-term interest rates low and signal clearly their intentions, rarely, if ever, disappointing the financial markets.

As Peter Warburton also points out, the scale of growth of the total world bond market over the past 20–30 years has been nothing short of incredible. His numbers show that the world bond market has exploded in size from US$3.3 trillion in 1980 to US$23.5 trillion outstanding by end-1997, comfortably surpassing the size of the total broad money supply of the OECD in the process. Between 1997 and 1999 new issuance in the international bond markets soared even further, the volume of new issuance almost doubling over these two years. Data produced by Salomon Smith Barney (Citigroup) show that the total public sector component of the outstanding global bond issue rose from US$2.1 trillion to US$13.3 trillion over the 1980 to 1997 period, an annualized rate of increase of 11.5 per cent. Government indebtedness has grown enormously, even as total tax burdens – particularly in the continental European countries – have also increased sharply.

The explosion in the size of the global bond market, and particularly of the public sector component, and the accompanying huge increase in measures of indebtedness, strongly suggests that the risk to investors in bonds has increased over the past 20 years. No doubt bond fund managers would argue that the sub-4 per cent yields to redemption on US 10-year Treasuries at the end of 2002 still promise a prospectively good real return to investors if the much talked-about threat of deflation proves a reality. But, in truth, deflation is merely a possibility, and a highly unlikely one at that. In Chapter 5 it will be argued that, contrary to current conventional wisdom, excessive indebtedness – particularly government indebtedness – is more likely to result in high inflation than the much feared 'debt deflation'. High levels of debt and the unsustainably rapid rate of growth of the securities markets suggest that investors should be requiring a higher compensation for the risk of investing in the securities markets, including in the bond markets.

So investors have seemingly acted to price the government bond markets, like the equity markets before them, as if they have become less risky when in fact they have become progressively more risky. How much more risky – in terms of what risk premium should be added to the true risk-free rate to arrive at an appropriate redemption yield (adjusted for inflation expectations) for long-term government debt – is probably impossible to assess. But the huge size of the markets, the potential for instability in the way in which much debt is held, and the greater risk of inflation consequent upon the increase in government indebtedness all argue for a higher risk premium than was normal in the past. In practice, given the same trend rate of economic growth, this would argue for a real interest rate, as implied in long-term government bond yields, higher than the 3.0–3.5 per cent that has been considered the historical norm.

Why have investors been prepared to buy government bonds at lower than normal real yields if, in fact, they are now more risky than in the past? The Warburton thesis amounts to a notion that central banks have accommodated (via monetary policy) and effectively underwritten institutional purchases of bonds. This is obviously rather similar to the analysis in Chapter 3 with regard to equity markets. In short, central bank policies have encouraged a bubble in both equity and bond markets. It is quite logical that, given the way markets function today, if there has been a giant bubble in one market there is also likely to have been a large bubble in the other. However, although the fact of the equity market bubble is now well recognized (because it has already been bursting), the equivalent bond bubble is not (because it has not begun to burst). If we look at who has been buying US Treasuries, then the big increase in ownership has been by foreign investors. According to Bridgewater Associates, foreign ownership of the US Treasury market had risen to 40 per cent of the outstanding market capitalization by 2002, up from under 20 per cent in 1995. The fact that foreigners now hold such a large proportion of the outstanding Treasury issue does not necessarily mean in itself that US government bond yields deserve a higher risk premium. But it obviously does imply a potential fault line that could play an important part in the eventual 'bond crash' that must surely occur one day.

It has already been mentioned that another possible explanation for the drop in real yields below historic norms that took place from 1995–96 onwards could be a drop in the trend growth rate of the world economy. Such a drop in trend growth would tend to occur very gradually – over a number of years – but would mean that instead of averaging an annual growth rate of 2.8 per cent, as it has over the past 30 years, in future real GDP for the OECD countries in aggregate might be set to average a lower rate of growth, say 2 per cent. It has to be admitted that this is highly plausible. Tax burdens in the European countries, in particular, are significantly higher than they were 30 years ago and higher tax burdens are probably the single most important negative influence on trend growth rates. In addition Japan, handicapped by an excessively regulated domestic economy and now stuck in a deflation, has been revealed to have a low trend growth rate and not the high trend growth rate that was once believed. On the other side of the ledger the US, by far the world's most important economy, is still believed by many to have achieved a higher trend rate of productivity growth and, therefore, overall economic growth. If this were true, it would offset the poorer outlook in continental Europe and Japan. Unfortunately, as discussed in Chapter 2, it is probably not true.

A fall to a lower trend growth rate seems to be a potential facilitating factor behind the creation of a financial bubble. It seems to have played a role in the Japanese stock market bubble of the late 1980s. There are three reasons – all of them involving a degree of irrationality on the part of participants in the financial markets and in the economy – why this might be so. First, a fall in trend growth means a tendency to a lower growth rate on average. If the central bank does not realize that the trend growth rate has fallen it will probably mistake the averagely lower growth numbers for cyclical weakness, therefore being encouraged to implement a looser monetary policy than actually appropriate. Second, if inflation is mis-measured – which it generally is – the fall in trend growth might, for a time, be associated with a lower measured rate of inflation, which would further persuade the central bank to maintain a loose policy and also encourage the markets. A fall in trend growth is a fall in demand growth and in supply growth, in aggregate, and therefore in theory it should have no effect on prices. However, as demand and supply growth fall there may be temporary disequilibria in different markets – for goods and services and for labour – that shift relative prices and impact inflation numbers, to the extent that there are measurement errors. Third, lower trend growth lowers the equilibrium real interest rate reflected in bond yields. Other things being equal bond yields should therefore fall. If equity investors do not recognize that the fall in bond yields reflects prospectively lower growth (and therefore lower real profits growth in future) then equity prices will rise.

This third reason brings us to a crucial point: that is, that even if the global trend growth rate has fallen it does not justify higher prices in the global equity market as a whole, even though it could be associated with lower bond yields. A very gradual fall in trend growth implies a very gradual fall in the equilibrium earnings yield for the market, as discussed before. Because the P/E ratio is the inverse of the earnings yield this implies that the equilibrium P/E ratio for the world market will be somewhat higher over time, but only because earnings are lower than they would have been if trend growth had remained at its previous level. In other words, lower trend growth will mean a lower trajectory of earnings, and as this emerges P/E ratios will tend to be somewhat higher in line with lower real bond yields. The equilibrium P/E ratio rises as earnings disappoint, not because stock prices rise. In this scenario bonds out-perform stocks. This is logical. It would not make sense to believe that stocks could perform well because world economic growth was going to be slower in the future than it had been in the past.

It is possible to argue, therefore, that a gradual decline in the world trend growth rate over the past five to ten years may have been an influence towards a lower level of real bond yields. However, the increased riskiness of bond markets, as the size of markets and levels of indebtedness have exploded, must be a factor working in the opposite direction on the equilibrium level of real bond yields. It is impossible – certainly at this time – to quantify these two elements but it seems highly unlikely, to say the least, that the fall in the trend growth rate could have been large enough, relative to the increase in risk, to bring about a fall in real bond yields of the magnitude that has been seen. The looseness of monetary policies, and the consequent high levels of liquidity in the global economy and in the US economy in particular, must have played an important role.

Peter Warburton's thesis is that central banks have created a kind of 'moral hazard' in bond markets by keeping short interest rates low and shying away from disappointing market expectations. This is another facet of loose monetary conditions. But it has only been possible for central banks to behave in this way and to keep monetary conditions loose for such a long period of time because measured inflation and, most importantly, inflation expectations, have not risen in response to sustained monetary expansion. Understanding why this has been possible is crucial to understanding how the markets will find their way back to long-run 'fair values', which is the topic of the next section of this chapter and of Chapter 5.

The Reversion to Fair Values

One of the City of London's most astute fund managers (Nick Train of investment boutique Lindsell Train) recognized in the 1990s that as the total capitalization of global financial markets was climbing ever higher, individual asset classes previously loved by fund managers were falling by the wayside, entering their own bear markets and leaving the global financial asset bull market concentrated in progressively fewer asset classes. First it was Japanese equities, then other Asian markets and emerging stock markets. Next he argued it would be the western stock markets, including the US stock market, that would fall away. In the end, he suggested, only the US Treasury bond would be left as the trusted repository of investors' funds.

This prediction deserved a wider audience than it received at the time because it has proved a pretty accurate simple roadmap for the way in which the long financial bull market developed. Successive hiccoughs and crises in different areas of the globe have encouraged central banks to maintain very loose monetary policies but the markets of the directly affected regions have never fully recovered. Instead excess global liquidity has been concentrated in fewer areas, and by 2002 this has meant mainly the government bond markets, which have as a result become grossly overvalued relative to a reasonable assessment of the prospects for inflation and the risk involved. However, this is not the end of the story as bonds will not remain permanently overvalued as government indebtedness continues to grow. There are other potential destinations for excess liquidity, including physical assets and commodities, and there is another monetary (and therefore effectively financial) asset that has not participated in the long liquidity-fuelled bull market. This is gold, which is discussed in the following chapter.

Over 2000–02 it has been the US equity market financial pyramid that has been unravelling. The force for this has not been tight liquidity but the interrelationships between the stock market and corporate earnings and the economy, as what had been the virtuous circle of feedback effects that characterized the financial bubble era became vicious. As stock prices declined, companies cut investment. The flow of initial public offerings dried up, further reducing business and encouraging further cutbacks in investment. Stock options became worthless, forcing companies to recognize their true cost base. Goodwill was written off as acquisitions made during the boom times proved to be worth less than had been believed. Pension fund surpluses disappeared to be replaced with deficits. Gains on corporate investment portfolios disappeared also. Investment banking earnings tumbled as the flow of mergers and acquisitions dried up, and fund management companies' revenues fell as stock markets slid. As corporate earnings fell, investors reacted by selling stocks further. As when a 'Ponzi scheme' turns bad, more and more investors feel the imperative to retrieve as much of their capital as they can. As more and more do this, the likelihood of those remaining in the scheme getting their money back becomes less and less, provoking more investors to try to get out. Once this process is ongoing, even very low interest rates and huge injections of liquidity into the economy by the central bank cannot really halt it, although these and other actions by the authorities may slow the process of collapse.

Bridgewater Associates has noted that during the US corporate earnings slump of 2000–01 one-time charges to earnings were running at an extraordinarily high level, equal to about a third of operating profits, or earnings before one-time charges. As a result, while operating earnings fell back to the levels that had first been reached in the mid-1990s, total net earnings, including one-time charges, crashed back to the levels of the early 1990s. One interpretation of this is that companies have taken the opportunity afforded by the poor economic environment to write off as much as possible, therefore establishing a low base from which future profits growth can easily be achieved. In late 2002 this benign interpretation was obviously the view of the market consensus. The S&P 500 remains extremely overvalued at a price-earnings multiple of around 30 based on current net earnings, but arguably somewhat more reasonable on a multiple of operating earnings, of about 20. Bridgewater also points, out that, going forward, analysts' expectations for corporate earnings remain very positive, with the aggregated expectation for operating earnings showing a return to the 1999 peaks during the course of 2003. If realized, this would place the S&P 500 in late 2002 on a prospective price–earnings ratio in line with the long-run average of 15–16 assuming that non-recurring charges fall to nothing or can safely be ignored.

This apparent market view presumes, in effect, that the cycle of boom and slump in stock market profits over 1994–2002 was simply a more severe form of the traditional cycle, from which a robust recovery can confidently be anticipated. Unfortunately, the pattern of feedback effects present in the fallout from a giant structural bubble such as this suggests that the hope for a robust profits recovery, from a position at which the stock market has never been clearly undervalued, is likely to prove forlorn. One possible piece of evidence pointing to a further decline in stock market profits is the divergence, over 1997–2002, between whole economy profits as reported in the US national accounts and the measures of stock market profits. National accounts profits peaked in 1997 and declined steeply until 2001. Notwithstanding the profits bounce-back over 2001–02, late in 2002 this measure of economic profits still stood more than 10 per cent below its 1997 peak levels. Stock market operating earnings for the companies in the S&P 500, on the other hand, soared during the climactic phase of the stock market bubble, over 1998–99, even as national accounts profits were flat or declining. Despite the huge decline in this measure of profits from the time of the stock market peak until early in 2001, late in 2002, and following a similar bounce-back, S&P operating earnings stood again above their 1997 levels. The correction in the stock market measure of operating earnings therefore looks less substantial than that in whole economy earnings, which suggests an incomplete bursting of the stock market-driven structural bubble (although, as noted previously, if the measure of profits considered is total net earnings, including one-time charges, then the decline in stock market earnings over 2000–01 was greater).

The market, including the stock analysts, essentially assumes that the underlying long-run trend in corporate earnings remains intact and all that has been witnessed is a big cycle around that trend. However, as has already been discussed above – and as will be explored further in the following chapters – the economic evidence is more consistent with a decline in global trend growth, and probably US trend growth also. It has also been noted that the formation of an asset bubble can tend to coincide with a decline in trend growth, which the bubble then exacerbates. If a decline in trend growth began coincident with the inception of the bubble in the mid-1990s, as the behaviour of real bond yields suggests, then the acceleration of earnings above trend from the mid-1990s until 1999 was of a greater magnitude than generally understood (because the long-run trend in real earnings is lower than presumed). By the same token the long-run trajectory to which real earnings will ultimately return is lower than the market discounts. This long-run trend path for earnings is impossible to know, and cannot be known until some years from now, but whatever it is the market was overvalued at the end of 2002 if the trend is indeed lower than the pre-1995 path. This is quite obvious from the numbers given above, which indicated that a rapid return to 1999 peak levels of operating earnings and an end to the unusually high level of one-time charges to earnings was needed to render the S&P 500 fair value, in the historic context, at end-2002.

For instance, assume that instead of quickly returning to peak levels, S&P 500 operating earnings return to a point midway between the 1999 peak and 2001 trough and that one-time charges fall to half their peak levels but still remain higher than usual. The resulting level of earnings placed on the long-run average price–earnings multiple of 15–16 would then point to a level for the S&P 500 of approximately 625, about one third lower than the levels of late 2002. Incidentally, this would return the S&P 500 back to the levels of early 1996, close to the beginnings of the bubble and making the sort of decline that should be a minimum expectation for a true 'bubble bursting'.

However, it would be difficult for most investors to conceive of a further stock market fall of this magnitude that did not result in even more damage to the economy, and consequently more damage to corporate earnings, and did not also result in a further huge rise in bond prices and therefore a further sharp decline in long yields. If we accept the analysis presented earlier, then bonds have also become very overvalued during the giant financial bubble and further declines in yields would only make them even more overvalued. Why should investors sell equities down to 'fair value' levels only to bid government bonds up to even more grossly overvalued levels? This would obviously not make much sense, and over 2000–02 it is precisely because bond yields have been so low, and apt to decline even further when equities have fallen steeply, that the falls in equity prices have been comparatively limited relative to the prior rise in equity prices, the collapse of corporate earnings, and the emergence of so much bad news concerning the economy and corporate sector.

This returns the argument to the subject of the previous chapter, namely liquidity. Although the actions of the Federal Reserve cannot ultimately prevent the unwinding of the structural bubble, they have clearly slowed the process. The maintenance of exceptionally loose liquidity in the economy has supported financial asset prices as a whole, meaning that equities' loss has been government bonds' gain. As long as inflation remains low then the Fed has the latitude to implement a monetary policy that results in a high rate of liquidity growth. As explained in the last chapter, if this policy proves to be compatible with low inflation, at least for a period, then by definition the demand for financial assets in aggregate, including money, must be high. If the demand for financial assets as a whole is strong then any significant fall in the demand for equities is going to be roughly matched by an increase in demand for other financial assets.

This situation cannot be sustainable indefinitely as has already been discussed in the previous chapters. The strong demand for US financial assets is associated with – and has to be associated with – strong demand for the US dollar. As we have seen, this implies growing imbalances in the US economy that must ultimately act to bring down the US dollar. In the end, either the dollar must decline substantially, undermining the demand for US financial assets including money and thereby stimulating inflation, or inflation must rise, with the same negative consequences for US financial assets and the dollar. The dollar issue is discussed in more depth in the following chapter. Suffice to say that it is easier to conceive of a substantial dollar decline if inflation in the rest of the world, particularly in Europe, is higher. A large dollar decline that occurred against a background of very low inflation globally could result in falls in goods' prices in the rest of the world, which would presumably prompt aggressive monetary easing outside the US. In a world in which the global institutions tend to see the dollar as the currency of choice, it would be difficult to imagine the markets selling the dollar considerably lower if this seemed likely to produce deflation outside the US.

However, if inflation is high enough in the rest of the world to accommodate a substantial dollar decline – or collapse even – without it causing overall consumer price inflation outside the US to fall negative, then such a decline in the US dollar becomes much more likely. With inflation higher, the latitude for the non-US central banks to ease policy aggressively is reduced, and the financial markets will be less likely to encourage such an easing. A consequent sharp decline in the dollar will of course be associated with rising inflation in the US also. If central banks outside the US loosen policy aggressively anyway, in order to support the dollar, then a self-reinforcing global inflationary cycle, similar to that which occurred in the 1970s, would be set in train.

Higher inflation would have the effect of eroding the liquidity excess because inflation reduces the real value of the money supply. It would also naturally lead to higher bond yields because bond investors would require to be compensated for higher inflation. But more than that, it would crystallize the higher risks that are already present in government bonds, resulting in a rise in real yields back up to a level that is more consistent with – and also probably well above – the prospective growth trend of the global economy. Higher real yields would also need to be reflected in a higher expected real return from equity markets in the future, meaning lower equity prices today. A higher risk premium – because inflation is higher – would probably also contribute to pulling down equity valuations. It is clearly through this inflationary route – and only through this route – that fair valuations of both stocks and bonds together, that would provide future investors with a viable real return from both asset classes over the long run, can be restored in an environment in which central banks are biased towards loose monetary policies. In late 2002 US government 10-year bonds, yielding around 4 per cent, are not going to provide investors with a viable real return in the long term. It is doubtful that today's investors will have to wait until the end of the 10 years to find this out.

At the end of 2002 the concern of most economic commentators is with the supposed threat of deflation, rather than inflation, and it is difficult for most financial market participants or corporate executives to take seriously the longer-run threat of inflation. As long as this climate of opinion persists then inflation expectations are, by definition, low and this in itself is an important contributor to sustaining a low inflation environment. However, the causal fundamentals point in the direction of inflation. Paul Ormerod, in his book on behavioural economics *Butterfly Economics*, discusses the potential for discontinuity in the inflation 'regime'. He argues that inflation can be thought of as being in one of two 'regimes': high or low. Writing in the 1990s his own conclusion is of a world in a low inflation regime typical of most of the history of capitalism. But one of the conclusions of this book is that, like pressure building up behind a leaky dam, the fundamental forces to inflation are growing and threatening to burst out, tipping the world quickly into a high-inflation regime. It will be when this occurs that the final correction in financial asset valuations to – or probably below – levels that have been more typical of history will take place. The fundamental causes and symptoms of this prospective inflation are the theme of the next chapter.

CHAPTER 5

Inflation or Deflation?

The Myth of Deflation

During – and even well before – the ongoing unwinding of the structural bubble in financial asset markets the great fear of market participants, most economists and policy makers alike has been deflation. In newspaper articles and much economic research the topic of 'deflation' has cropped up again and again, each time as if it is a new and horrifying possibility that has just emerged on the economic horizon. As the general economic environment has changed, the arguments presented by the 'deflationists' have changed accordingly. In 1998 and 1999 the explosive growth of the internet – bringing forth much greater competition – and an accompanying surge in productivity supposedly represented a deflationary threat. Over 2000–02 fears turned to 'debt deflation' as the stock market bubble began to unwind. This scaremongering about deflation has appeared credible to many people because in the background measured inflation has remained low. But it is notable that, over the period during which deflation stories have been prevalent, inflation outside Japan (which has been experiencing genuine deflation) has generally been above, rather than below, prior expectations. This fact has not deterred the 'deflationists' from persisting with warnings of imminent deflationary disaster.

The investment banks have remained particularly convinced of the case for very low inflation or even deflation. In December 1999 Morgan Stanley Dean Witter's European strategist wrote, 'At no point in the next three years do we expect the ECB's (European Central Bank) 2 per cent upper inflation limit to be breached' (*Morgan Stanley Dean Witter UK and Europe Investment Research*, 2 December 1999). In the three years subsequent to this, widely shared, prediction only for two or three months has inflation actually been within the ECB's supposed limit. Yet economists have persisted in arguing that the ECB's policy has been too tight to the extent of risking deflation. This deflation view has been close to a consensus amongst the investment banks, and also other financial economists, since 1998. In November 1998 Crédit Suisse First Boston economists, also commenting on Europe, wrote, 'If anything, the greatest risk appears to be a "deflation spiral", particularly in sectors exposed to external competition' (Crédit Suisse First Boston, *Euro-11 Economics Weekly*, 20 November 1998). Robert Fleming strategists asserted in the introduction to an investment research piece in January 1999, 'For Europe, the question is no longer whether deflation will happen, but rather what type of deflation will it be. The risk of the deflation turning to depression is greater in continental Europe than in the US or even the UK' (Flemings Research Europe, *Surviving deflation*, 27 January 1999). In February 1999 respected US economist Ed Hyman was arguing that 'deflation [is] closer than most realize'.

The financial press has taken the same tack, resurrecting deflation stories every so often over the past five years. A Reuters news agency article at the end of 1998 began: 'The year is ending as it began, with the world's top central bankers confronting the spectre of a destructive downward spiral in prices' (Reuters, 8 December 1998). At the time Reuters was polling economists on the question 'How will the ECB tackle the deflation threat?' In February 1999 both *The Economist* and *Institutional Investor* magazine chose to run cover stories on deflation, *The Economist* with deflation as 'The new danger' and *Institutional Investor* with 'Deflation – It's closer than you think'. The *Financial Times* took the same line. Like Morgan Stanley, in December 1999 the *Financial Times* asserted, 'inflation (in the Eurozone) will still almost certainly be below the ECB's highest acceptable level of 2 per cent' (7 December 1999). A year earlier, in December 1998, in a leader titled 'Oiling the wheels of deflation', the *Financial Times* had argued that 'Prices (of commodities) have been falling so sharply that they may also herald another danger – that of cumulative deflation' (12 December 1998). In November 2001 the *Financial Times* were arguing that the 'Spectre of deflation spooks economists' (13 November 2001), and they were still making the deflation case a year later.

Faced with this constant barrage of deflation predictions from the media and the financial community it is not surprising that politicians and policy makers have been influenced to think in the same way. In November 1998 Bank of Italy Governor Antonio Fazio claimed that inflation had now been defeated and that the new enemy was unemployment. In early 1999 the then German Finance Minister Oskar Lafontaine was warning against the possibility of deflation and urging the ECB to cut interest rates, while in March of that year soon-to-be European Commission President Romano Prodi warned in a speech, 'We have to beware of price deflation and be ready to adopt, in the EU, the proper policies to shun the disruptive effect of a generalized fall of prices.' In its annual report in June 1999 the Bank for

International Settlements (BIS), the 'central bankers' central bank', posited that global prices were more likely to fall than rise, despite strong growth in some economies. With this climate of opinion, it is easy to understand why central banks were comfortable to maintain interest rates at low levels and keep the global economy very well-supplied with liquidity.

Throughout these five years of virtually continuous predictions of impending deflation, measured consumer price inflation rates in the western economies have actually remained comparatively stable at fairly low levels. In the US inflation has oscillated between 1 per cent and 4 per cent, in the Eurozone between 0.5 per cent and 3.5 per cent, and in the UK between 0.5 per cent and 4 per cent. These inflation rates are comparatively low, certainly by the standards of the post-war period, but do not represent deflation and have most of the time been tending to exceed the prior forecasts of economists, as would be evident from some of the quotes given above. This has not dissuaded those economists and other financial commentators who believe in the imminence of deflation from continuing to press their case. Whenever the failure of prior predictions of deflation is discussed – which is rarely – then the failure of prices to plunge is generally attributed to 'one-off shocks' such as oil price increases or the BSE and foot-and-mouth food crises. To non-believers in deflation this looks like a case of 'I've made up my mind – don't confuse me with the facts.'

If the 'deflationists' have made up their mind, then what is it that has made them so certain? As mentioned earlier, the arguments have changed as the economic environment has changed over the past few years but a number of elements in the deflation story have remained fairly constant, so it is worth discussing these briefly in turn.

Declines in Goods' Prices Because of New Sources of Global Supply

Articles on the risk of deflation invariably note that the prices of clothing and some manufactured goods have been falling steeply because of greater supply from low labour cost countries such as China, which are increasingly important competitors in the global market for goods. There is no doubt that this is true as far as it goes. The very long-term chart in Figure 5.1, for instance, shows that prices for apparel in the US have been on a trend decline relative to price levels in general ever since the global economy began to become more open to trade in the 1970s. In percentage terms this relative price fall has become even greater in recent years. What is wrong with this argument, however, is that such price declines for categories of goods consequent upon changes in supply conditions for those goods are, in the end,

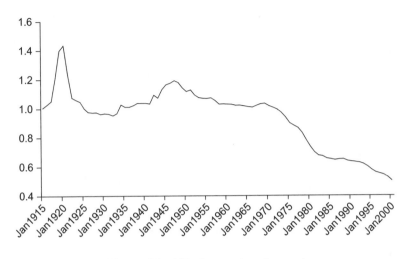

Figure 5.1 US relative price of apparel

changes in *relative* prices not changes in overall price levels in the economy. If China, for instance, is supplying more goods to the global market as it has become more open to trade, eventually it will be demanding more goods and services from the rest of the world also. It will not be able to run a larger and larger trade and current account surplus indefinitely without eventually experiencing inflation or currency revaluation, either of which would act to undermine the competitiveness of its exports. More likely, as the Chinese economy grows, China will be demanding goods and services from the rest of the world that it does not produce itself, raising global demand in these areas.

The UK, for instance, has experienced a particularly large decline in clothing and footwear prices over recent years, this decline becoming a key component of a fall in overall shop prices for goods. However, services' price rises have accelerated, with service price inflation reaching nearly 5 per cent late in 2002. The overall inflation environment has remained fairly stable and within that overall stability it is relative prices that have shifted.

Greater Competition in the World Economy Because of Globalization

An often heard argument for deflation is that companies face greater competitive pressures than in the past, meaning that they cannot raise prices and therefore there cannot be any inflation. During the internet bubble, the internet and the new technologies were supposed to be adding to this increase in competition. Leaving aside the fact that competition has always been assumed in classical economic theory and no respectable economic theory ever claimed that there could never be inflation as long as there was competition, it is doubtful that the assertion of greater competition globally is actually true. In many industries, large companies now find themselves operating in oligopolistic conditions, with two or three major competitors globally. In the short run this could give rise to brutal price competition but the long-run outcome is more likely to be industries operating implicitly as cartels, with resulting inefficiency creating a fertile ground for inflationary pressures to take root.

The growth of global oligopolies has been a legacy of the 'merger mania' of the 1990s, which became more intense in parallel with the overall stock market mania. On 23 November 1998 a record was set when eight deals worth more than US$1 billion were announced in a single day. Plenty more followed in 1999 when the total value of global mergers set a new record, hitting US$2.2 trillion for just the first nine months of that year. Even as it was taking place, this merger frenzy provoked concerns in some quarters that stood in contradiction to the prevailing wisdom that competition glob-ally was becoming more intense. In a March 1999 front-page article entitled 'Let's Play Oligopoly! It's a Favourite Pursuit of Corporate Giants', the *Wall Street Journal* aired some of these concerns (10 March 1999). In a separate analysis, economists at Crédit Suisse First Boston wrote, in October 1999,

> 'Ultimately, the process of mega-mergers might lead to something analo-gous to the trusts of the 1890s, or the government-sanctioned cartels of the 1960s, committed to closing capacity and forcing prices up by restrict-ing supply. Getting rid of competitors in this way is great for ensuring that companies keep all the benefits from the research they do, rather than having them competed away. But as we saw in the 1960s, it is also a recipe for channelling technological development into ever-narrower areas and also for fostering inflation.' (Crédit Suisse First Boston, Fixed Income Research Europe, 'Ten Questions for the Millennium', 22 October 1999)

Greater Productivity and Improving Quality of Goods

Another argument often made for deflation is that ongoing improvements in productivity will depress unit labour costs and keep prices under pressure. It is often also claimed that inflation statistics do not adequately capture the improving quality of goods and that prices would already be declining in the west if quality improvements were properly taken into account.

The productivity argument is wrong in theory and also in practice. First, it is only in the US where there are grounds for believing that the productivity growth trend has risen in recent years. The case for disputing this apparent improvement in the productivity trend was made in Chapter 2. In continental Europe, in particular, productivity growth appears to have deteriorated. Second, and as also discussed in Chapter 2, if there really had been a long-run improvement in the labour productivity trend, in the end the benefits would fall to labour, in the form of higher real wages. But this rise in real wages would only occur via a fall in prices if the monetary authority failed to recognize the improvement in the productivity trend and therefore failed to accommodate it in its monetary policy. Higher trend productivity growth means higher trend economic growth. This does not have implications for prices unless the authorities make policy errors.

The view that improvements in the general quality of goods were being inadequately accounted for in official inflation statistics (that is inflation statistics were incorporating price increases that were really payments for improved quality) was given credibility by the Boskin Commission, a commission headed by Stanford University economist Michael Boskin that was tasked with investigating inadequacies in the US inflation data, and reported in 1996. The Boskin Commission estimated that US consumer price inflation statistics overestimated the true inflation rate by as much as 1.1 per cent annually as a result of a number of factors including quality improvement and the belated introduction of new products into the statistics, as well as the failure to take adequate account of consumers' ability to substitute products with rising prices for similar products and products bought at different outlets, such as discount stores. As a result of the Commission's findings, changes have been made to the way the US consumer price index is calculated, which have amounted to roughly a 0.5 per cent reduction in the measured inflation rate relative to the rate that would have been calculated using the pre-1996 methodology.

The Boskin Commission findings have been generally accepted and some of its recommendations have also been adopted in other countries. The German Statistics Office has started to apply the hedonic price measurement method – which effectively views goods in terms of the services they provide to the buyer over time – to take account of quality improvements in items such as computers and cars. Although it is undeniably true that the quality of products such as computers, cars, hi-fi equipment, communications equipment and so on has been improving considerably, similar quality improvements also took place in the past to other products that were benefiting from advancing technology. Making adjustments to today's statistics to take account of improving quality may make today's statistics a more accurate guide to the true inflation rate but they will mislead insofar as suggesting a relative improvement in inflation when compared with the past (when the statistics were not being similarly adjusted).

Furthermore, in the view of this author (a view also shared by other critics of the Boskin Commission findings) the idea that the quality of most goods and services is inexorably improving seems a little rose-coloured. Where the Boskin Commission had no clear evidence for quality improvements it assumed zero change in quality. In no broad category of goods or services did it allow for the possibility of declining quality. This seems at odds with personal experience of modern living. Low prices have sometimes been achieved at the cost of lower quality of service, for instance when personal service is replaced by call centres or automated telephone-answering systems. Even for goods, lower prices sometimes mean a shorter useful life (for example clothing, light bulbs). In the case of cars, it is taken for granted that quality has improved because of the inclusion of all the modern computer gadgetry that now comes as standard in modern cars. But it would be hard to persuade the driver caught in the endless traffic gridlock of major cities such as London or Los Angeles that the benefits of car ownership have been continuously improving. In London, notoriously, estimates suggest that the average speed of road travel is now lower than it was a century ago, in the age of the horse and carriage. The Londoner resorting to public transport instead will not find that he or she is benefiting from a continuous improvement in quality there, either.

To this, possibly rather cynical, author, changes to the measurement of inflation statistics to make them accord more with the conventional wisdom that there is no inflation looks a little like trying to adjust the facts to fit a preconceived view rather than building a view based on the facts.

Weak Commodity Prices

Particularly in 1998, when commodity prices had been in sharp decline, it was often suggested that a long secular decline in commodity prices would put downward pressure on global prices generally. In a report released in early 1999 the World Bank argued that the long history of relative declines in commodity prices would continue thanks to production-boosting advances in technology enabling the mining and production of new supplies of commodities more cheaply than in the past. It is interesting to note how far consensus opinion has changed since the 1970s, when most believed that commodities were 'running out' and that the economics of exhaustible resources meant that commodity prices would have to rise in real terms by enough to force economies in their usage and a search for substitutes.

The commodity price argument for deflation is a poor one as best demonstrated by how quickly believers in deflation change arguments when commodity prices are rising, such as during 2002. Then rising commodity prices are advanced as a reason to expect weak demand and weak growth – and therefore ultimately lower general price pressures – because of the negative impact of rising commodity prices on real incomes in the commodity-consuming countries.

Weak Demand and Excess Capacity in the Global Economy

Perhaps the most common argument for deflation is the idea that the global economy is beset by excess production capacity and that global demand has not been strong enough to allow this capacity to be utilized, with downward pressure on prices being the inevitable result. The idea that there is excess global capacity derives from consideration of the huge amount of investment that took place during the stock market bubble, surveys of companies which suggest that they are operating at low levels of capacity utilization, and the observation that global output is below the level that should be expected based on its long-run trend (that is 'output gap' analysis). The problem with this view, and with these measures of excess capacity, is that they ignore the implications of the financial bubble. As has been discussed previously in this book, asset bubbles lead to the misallocation of resources and investment that ultimately proves redundant. Therefore standard measures of capacity utilization will tend to show excess capacity during the unwinding of a bubble, but much of this excess capacity may prove useless, as the eventual recovery of demand in the economy is likely to be, at least in part, in areas that were not the object of investment during the bubble. Furthermore, output gap analysis may also be misleading if the formation of the bubble and its unwinding is associated with a reduction in the trend rate of growth, as has also previously been suggested as likely.

Debt Deflation

Since the stock market bubble burst, the focus of deflation concerns has been on the issue of debt deflation. This issue has been touched upon in Chapter 3. It is also somewhat related to the issue of excess capacity, discussed above. 'Debt deflation' occurs when debtors react to falling prices and asset values by seeking to repay debts, the burden of which rises in real terms as prices fall. In order to repay loans, debtors will tend to sell assets, resulting in further asset price deflation. The potential is then for a vicious circle of credit contraction and asset price deflation.

However, for a debt deflation such as this to take hold, money supply and bank credit must be contracting. In Japan's post-bubble deflation, for instance, bank credit has been contracting by as much as −4 per cent to −5 per cent annually. If money and credit are not contracting it is not possible for a vicious circle of deflation to take hold. As already explained in Chapter 3, deepening deflation without monetary contraction would imply a continuous rise in the demand for money. While risk aversion on the part of investors might allow for some rise in the demand for money relative to the norm, an abnormally rising trend in the demand for money could not be sustained indefinitely on this basis.

In the western economies money and credit have not been contracting. In fact they have been growing rather strongly. Those who worry about debt deflation would argue that this does not mean that such a credit contraction and deflation could not occur in the future. They would point to historically high levels of indebtedness across the western world, and in the US in particular, as indicating the risk. In the US, by the end of the 1990s both corporate debt and consumer debt had reached record levels relative to the size of the economy. In very rough numbers, and using the most widely used data, total consumer debt was about equal to total personal disposable income by the end of 1999, and non-financial corporate debt was close to 50 per cent of GDP, both record amounts. Total private debt (business and consumer) was over 130 per cent of GDP, also a record. In the US (not elsewhere) government debt relative to GDP was declining during the late 1990s because of the large budget surpluses, but it was still over 50 per cent of GDP at the end of the decade. This produced a total debt ratio of approximately 180 per cent, a historically very high level that had been sustained during the 1990s. Looking forward, the US government budget is now moving into large deficit which means that, as government debt begins to grow again, the total debt ratio could begin a renewed upward climb.

There is little question that debt levels are excessive across the world (in Japan it is public debt which is a huge problem). However, it is far from clear that this means deflation is inevitable. On the contrary, in the past extreme indebtedness has been just as likely to be associated with high inflation as with deflation. There is a good reason for this. Economies tend to be self-correcting. Deflation will make a problem of excessive indebtedness worse because the burden of servicing the debt will be rising in real terms as prices fall. It is inflation that is the 'cure' for excessive debt.

Some economists would make the distinction between government and private debt when it comes to considering the issue of inflation versus deflation. Historically, when countries have experienced hyperinflations this has usually been associated with out-of-control government deficits and debt. If government deficits become effectively unfinanceable the temptation to monetize the deficit and debt (that is to create central bank money to finance the deficit) is obvious. But even in modern financial systems where it is not possible for governments to finance deficits by 'printing money' in such a blatant and inflationary way, there can still be pressures towards indirect monetization of deficits – leading to inflation – if the government deficit and debt level becomes so large as to threaten financial stability. In this eventuality markets will tend to begin building a greater risk premium into long-term government bond yields, reflecting the burden of government financing and the risk it poses. As this pressure towards higher real yields transmits down the yield curve, then the central bank will find itself tending to inject more liquidity into the banking system in order to keep short-term interest rates at the targeted level. Therefore money and credit will tend to accelerate as the banking sector will be funded by the central bank to buy higher-yielding government debt (creating money in the process) unless the central bank is prepared to allow a concomitant rise in short-term interest rates (to match the rise in government bond yields).

One argument, therefore, is that excessive government debt tends to lead to inflation (because of pressures towards the monetization of debt) but excessive private sector debt can pose a deflationary risk (because of the risk of debt deflation). However, this distinction is probably false. Just as with government deficits and debt, large private sector deficits and debt burdens can place strains on the economy that prompt the central bank to be accommodative with its monetary policy, thereby encouraging inflation. This has already been demonstrated in the case of the US. As noted in Chapter 2, the increasing stress on the economy created by the burgeoning private sector financial deficit and debt burden in the late stages of the stock market bubble was associated with a sharp widening of credit spreads (the difference between corporate bond yields and government bond yields). When these spreads ballooned out following the Russian default and LTCM crisis in 1998, the Fed used this as a reason to ease monetary policy sharply. The reality is that in a modern financial system, based on fiat money and central banks with discretion over monetary policy, debt is more likely to be associated with inflation, ultimately because an inflationary path is the path of least resistance on the route to bringing the debt burden under control in real terms.

Why Has Inflation Remained Low?

Up to now this chapter has been concerned with demonstrating that the arguments commonly advanced for an incipient global deflation are without foundation. On the contrary, it has already been argued in this book (in Chapter 3) that the development of the financial bubble and the authorities' response to its gradual unwinding has in fact been associated with an economic environment in the western world that is fundamentally inflationary. The clearest evidence for this is found in continuing high rates of money growth and exceptionally loose central bank policies. Inflation is by definition a fall in the value (or price) of money, while deflation is a rise in the value, or price, of money. If money is going to be rising in value (deflation) even as its supply is increasing sharply, then the law of supply and demand dictates that it must be experiencing sharply increasing demand (that is the demand for money must be rising strongly). In Chapter 3 it was explained that such a situation of strong money demand could be expected to occur during a bubble in financial assets, but that it could not be a permanent situation. In the end, if the supply of money continues to increase sharply the value of money will fall.

If global financial and economic developments have been fundamentally inflationary, why has inflation globally actually remained low, lending ongoing credibility to forecasts of eventual deflation? The argument that the financial bubble itself created strong demand for money and thereby helped to suppress inflation – relative to the rapid growth of money supply – is rather circular, given that the bubble itself could only come about because inflation remained low. There must have been other forces at work that have reinforced the tendency to low global inflation.

The key is inflation expectations. Economists have known for decades that expectations for inflation have a huge influence over actual inflation outcomes. At a time of a sea change in the fundamental inflation environment, expectations can initially change more slowly than warranted and then catch up with reality more rapidly later. Following the highly inflationary 1970s, expectations that high inflation could return remained stubborn despite the aggressively tight monetary policies implemented by central banks at the beginning of the 1980s. As a result, through much of the 1980s measured real interest rates tended to remain high and central banks were forced to maintain short rates at comparatively high levels to bear down on credit demand, which was still stimulated by an inflationary psychology. By the end of 2002, in complete contrast, the psychology was entirely 'disinflationary' or deflationary. Central banks are able to maintain interest rates at very low levels without credit demand becoming completely out of control. Possible reasons for the low level of real long-term interest rates have been discussed previously, but clearly another potential cause of low *measured* real rates is simply that market participants are building into bond pricing an expected future rate of inflation that is below the current and recent past inflation rate. These inflation expectations can be stubborn and self-perpetuating for a time, with the type of phenomena discussed above – falling prices of some manufactured goods because of new sources of supply, for instance – helping to keep inflation expectations down. Other factors previously discussed – such as lower trend growth possibly resulting in a temporarily lower-measured inflation rate – could also play a part. If inflation expectations remain stubbornly low, this will obviously help the central banks keep the actual inflation rate low in the short-to-medium term. But, by the same token, if fundamental inflation pressures are building up it increases the risk of policy errors by the central banks.

In *Butterfly Economics* (see p. 3) Paul Ormerod argues that inflation can be in one of two regimes, high or low. The interaction between the expectations of the different participants in the economy and the relationship between expectations and outcomes implies the possibility of 'discontinuity', whereby there is a comparatively rapid change from one regime to the other. Although expectations are stubborn, once things do begin to change they can eventually change quite quickly as various factors act to reinforce each other and reinforce the change in expectations.

There are two factors – or prices – which could be particularly relevant in the current environment and could eventually play a role in shifting the regime from the low inflation regime of the 1990s to a new high inflation regime more like that of the 1970s. These two factors are the price of gold and the price of the dollar in terms of the major foreign currencies. To monetary purists these are merely aspects of the same thing – the price, or value, of the US money stock. The US dollar price of gold (or more precisely its inverse) represents the value of US money in terms of an absolute standard of value, while the dollar in terms of foreign currencies represents the value of US money relative to foreign monies. An incipient US inflation ought to be apparent in the dollar falling in terms of gold (gold going up) and the dollar falling in terms of foreign currencies. However, it will be argued below that in the present incipient inflation various forces have come into play that have tended to prevent this happening, and in so doing have reinforced each other and thereby reinforced the tendency for inflation expectations to remain low. Once these factors have broken down, a large slide in the dollar and sharp rise in the gold price will help move the world to a high inflation regime that is more in keeping with the long prior period of loose monetary policies.

Gold

Gold has an extremely long history as a money, with the advantage of a relatively stable supply curve in the short term that is outside the control of central banks, meaning that it can, in theory, be used as a measure of value of other monies. For instance, if the gold price is low and falling in dollar terms then the value of US money is high and rising in terms of gold, in theory pointing to deflation. If other currencies are persistently falling in dollar terms (that is the dollar is rising in the foreign exchange markets) then this could be sending the same message, but alternatively it could be that inflationary policies are being pursued outside the US, rather than because of deflationary US policies. In other words, to the extent that currency exchange rates contain information about the value of money the information is of a relative nature. Gold is capable of being a more absolute indicator of the value of money, at least over the long term. Both gold and currency exchange rates suffer from being influenced by non-monetary factors over the short-to-medium term, but this is probably a bigger problem for currencies than for gold most of the time. That having been said, the real price of gold has been subject to some substantial fluctuations over the past century, and this issue is discussed below.

If gold can serve as an indicator of the value – or price – of money then the gold price in real terms should be relatively stable over time. As mentioned in Chapter 3, the price of money is the inverse of the general price level of goods and services because the value of money is ultimately represented by the goods and services that money can buy. Therefore, if gold can serve as a measure of the value of money its price must move roughly in line with the general price level, meaning that in real terms (that is deflated by an index of prices such as the consumer price index) the gold price must be fairly stable over time. Figure 5.3 shows that in broad terms this has been true, at least for data covering the last 130 years. (It is somewhat less true over a longer time span, when large gold discoveries had an impact.) The fact that the price of gold tends to be fairly stable in real terms over the very long term puts gold in a strange position in the spectrum of investable assets.

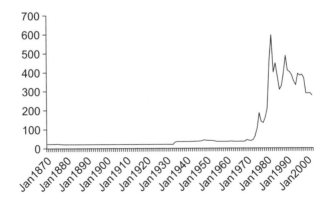

Figure 5.2   Gold price annually 1870–2000

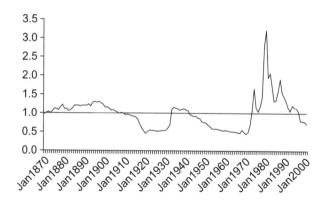

Figure 5.3 Real price of gold

To the extent that it is a monetary asset it could be considered a financial asset. However, the fact that its price tends to move with the general price level makes it more like a real asset (such as property), in practice, albeit one that over the very long run provides no real return to investors. Central banks can earn a return by lending gold (discussed below) but for most long-term gold investors the attraction of holding gold is not the return, but the security that derives from holding the safest of all assets, an asset for which there is no corresponding liability.

During the inflationary 1970s, gold (and other commodities also) became the object of extreme speculation, and gold became severely overvalued during a speculative bubble that peaked in January 1980 when its price exceeded US$800 per ounce. Subsequently, gold entered a 20-year secular bear market that ended (in the opinion of this author) when the price fell close to US$250 per ounce in July–August 1999 (albeit that this level was nearly revisited over February–April 2001). In the latter stages of this bear market the view became fashionable that gold had lost its monetary properties and become 'just another commodity'. This view was given weight, in the opinion of most commentators at the time, by central banks' sales of gold from their reserves. Central banks in aggregate had been selling gold since 1995 but central bank sales became particularly high-profile when the Bank of England announced, in May 1999, its intention to more than half its gold holdings, selling roughly 400 tonnes of gold in a sequence of bi-monthly auctions. The Bank of England's decision to sell gold followed closely an announcement by the Swiss central bank of its intention also to sell about half of its gold reserves – about 1,300 tonnes. The Swiss sales have been conducted through the BIS at a rate of about 200 tonnes per year, while the Bank of England's gold auction programme was finally completed in March 2002.

Consensus opinion was that these sales of gold from official reserves represented the final nail in the coffin of gold's status as a monetary asset. Articles about gold in the UK edition of the *Financial Times*, subtitled respectively: 'Gold no longer has an official role as money and may yet end up as just another commodity so the price it will eventually command is far from clear' (14 June 1999), and 'Commodity's role as global monetary reserve has been replaced by dollar' (13 October 2000), reflected this sentiment. However, the notion that gold's monetary status depended exclusively on the whims of a number of central bankers and government ministers, such as UK Chancellor of the Exchequer Gordon Brown, was frankly ludicrous. Gold's status as a money has a history that is centuries old whereas, by comparison, today's global monetary system, built purely upon fiat monies, dates back only to the Second World War. Even under the Bretton Woods system of fixed exchange rates (1947–73) gold still had a role in that central banks were able to convert dollars into gold at a fixed rate (of US$35 per ounce) with the US monetary authorities, a constraint that helped prevent the Federal Reserve from expanding the supply of dollars (which served as the anchor for the system) too quickly. This role was terminated on 15 August 1971 when President Richard Nixon closed the gold window. In the subsequent 30 years of pure fiat money, inflation has averaged a much higher rate than in previous history, meaning that it is much too early to make judgements about the sustainability of the current global monetary regime, or the end of gold's monetary status.

Another of the many negative arguments for gold that emerged during the long bear market was the idea that the value of gold would inevitably be undermined by the existence of the large above-ground holdings, estimated (by Gold Fields Mineral Services) to total in excess of 140,000 metric tons. It is often pointed out (as a negative argument for gold) that most of the gold ever produced still exists, therefore supposedly representing an overbearing weight of 'supply'. This opinion is another that stems from a complete misunderstanding of the characteristics from which gold derives its monetary status. The fact that gold does not decay or perish is one of the important characteristics that have led to its being used as a money throughout history (others being its scarcity and its malleability). A little counter-example can serve to illuminate this point. In countries suffering hyperinflation at various times in the past, cigarettes have been known to serve as a form of money. In the case of cigarettes, it is certainly not true that most of the historic production still exists; in fact only a fraction of all the cigarettes ever produced is in existence today. Yet this does not mean that there is a 'lack of supply' that somehow makes cigarettes a better form of money, even in a hyperinflation. It is gold's permanence that enables it to serve as a store of value, which is one of the characteristics of a money, and from which it derives its value.

It is certainly conceivable that one day, far in the future, gold could lose completely its nature as a monetary asset and become 'just another commodity', as so many argued during gold's 20-year bear market. But that day is not today. Gold's history as a money is simply too long to be nullified by just a few years of low inflation and dollar strength. This means that we can still use gold as a monetary indicator, albeit with considerable caution because of the possibility that gold's real value can be influenced by non-monetary factors over the short-to-medium term.

The earlier chart of the real price of gold shows that the period beginning in the mid-1990s has been one of three extended periods of depressed real gold prices in the past 130 years, the other two being the periods 1920–33 and 1952–70. The first of these periods was the era of the gold exchange standard when currencies were fixed to gold at what proved to be too low a price for gold (too high a level for currencies). This helped to create a classic deflationary environment, in which monetary conditions were squeezed in order for general price levels to be forced into consistency with the low price fixed for gold. This deflation only ended when gold was revalued in 1933. During the 1920s and 1930s deflation, therefore, the price of gold accurately signalled deflationary conditions in the economy. This was not the case in the second episode, however. During this, Bretton Woods, period the link between gold and global monetary conditions was much less rigid because only central banks had the right freely to convert dollars into gold at a fixed rate. It was possible for the monetary policies pursued by the central banks as a whole (led by the US Fed) to become gradually incompatible with the fixed dollar price for gold, as indeed happened during the 1960s and early 1970s. The culmination of this divergence between a low fixed price for gold and expansive monetary policies being pursued by the Fed and other central banks was the subsequent suspension of the gold window and the soaring gold price of the 1970s.

In this second episode, therefore, a low real price of gold was not indicative of an incipient deflation – in fact the reverse was the case: it was an inflation that followed. The key is that during the 1960s the price of gold was being pegged by central banks but, unlike under the gold standard or gold exchange standard, there was not a strong link from gold to monetary conditions. Arguably, this period provides a better precedent for the situation in the 1990s, when central bank involvement in the gold market was also significant, but in a way that had no direct influence upon monetary policies or monetary conditions. Central bank sales of gold from official reserves – estimated to total about 300 tonnes a year net since 1995 (more towards the end of the 1990s) – are, in effect, 'sterilized intervention'. To monetary economists, this means intervention in the markets (usually for currencies) that can affect prices in these markets temporarily but should have no lasting impact because the central bank ensures that overall monetary conditions are left unaffected by the activity.

In the case of this sterilized intervention in gold the amounts relative to the size of the market have been significant. Net sales of 300–400 tonnes a year equal 10–15 per cent of annual new mined supply of approximately 2,500 tonnes, enough to have an impact, at least initially, until the market adjusts to the new source of supply. However, central bank activity in the gold market has been much greater than suggested merely by figures for net sales. Central banks have been very active in the market for lending gold, lending gold from their reserves that provides the ultimate backing for short positions held by those who wish to speculate on a declining gold price, or hedge against the risk of price declines. In simple terms the way this works is that central banks lend gold from reserves to earn a modest return. The borrowers of this gold can sell the borrowed gold in the spot market so that they then have a 'short' position, and stand to profit from a gold price decline, following which they would be able to buy back the gold more cheaply. Investment banks (the bullion banks) can use such gold borrowings to help offset risks they assume in derivatives positions and structures that they create for gold mining companies who wish to hedge against the risk of future gold price declines.

Typically it would be gold producers that would be expected to use such methods to cover the risk of future gold price declines. They own reserves of gold in the ground, and to prevent these diminishing in value they might want to 'lock in' a price for some of the reserves through forward sales or by using derivatives or gold borrowings. Towards the end of the gold bear market, in the late 1990s, such hedging by miners became rampant, as it looked more and more likely to most observers that the gold price was going to continue dropping. Gold Fields Mineral Services estimated that new producer hedging totalled a net 445 tonnes in 1999, equivalent to 15–20 per cent of annual mined supply. Additionally they estimated that the total of such gold loan-backed hedges (or outright 'short positions') outstanding at that time was around 5,000 tonnes, equal to two years of mined supply. The problem inherent in this situation was perfectly illustrated in 1999, following an agreement announced on 26 September of that year under which 15 European central banks agreed collectively to freeze gold lending and limit gold sales to a total of 400 tonnes per year for the following five years. A scramble to cover short positions in the gold market triggered an unprecedented surge in the gold price, of about 30 per cent in a week, which nearly bankrupted two mining companies – Ashanti and Cambior – that had 'over-hedged'. The problem is that the gold reserves are in the ground whereas the hedges are financial contracts that may require margin, or other funds, to be placed against them in the event of becoming heavily 'offside'. In the case of a fully hedged position, the miner's exposure to the gold price will be neutral in the sense that in the event of a rise in the gold price the increasingly negative value of the financial contract is offset by the rise in the value of the reserves in the ground. But the gold in the ground is not liquid while the increased financial liability may need to be supported with additional margin, threatening a liquidity problem, as was indeed faced by Ashanti.

During the bear market those borrowing gold and selling it, or using derivatives backed by such selling, were not only miners but also speculators of various types. By all accounts a gold 'carry trade', similar to the popular yen carry trade, had become a popular strategy for hedge funds and other long/short investors by the late stages of the gold bear market. Because the cost of borrowing gold from the central banks is low, hedge funds could borrow gold, sell it, and then use the funds acquired to finance positions in financial markets. This was hugely profitable for as long as gold continued to fall in price because the funds were making money on gold falling as well as on financial markets rising. By selling gold from reserves and making it clear that they saw gold as a poor investment, central banks were effectively countenancing these trades. They appeared to be underwriting short gold positions while simultaneously underwriting stock markets (see Chapter 3). It is not surprising that the magnitude of short-selling in gold became so great, mirroring the intensity of speculation in stock markets.

It is likely that the bulk of short positions in the gold market – whether speculative or hedging by mining companies – would ultimately correspond to gold borrowed from the central banks. This would be true unless bullion banks were prepared to issue uncovered derivatives, thereby exposing themselves to huge risks, which would be unlikely on any significant scale. There has been much controversy about the scale of central bank gold lending. In August 2001 a senior official at the BIS gave an estimate that around 5,200 tonnes of gold had been lent to the market – equivalent to about two years of mined supply – roughly confirming the more conservative private estimates.

An active group of conspiracy theorists, calling themselves the Gold Anti-Trust Action Committee (GATA), have claimed that the scale of gold lending is much greater than that admitted to by the central banks, in excess of 11,000 tonnes according to their estimates. They further argue that the magnitude of the accompanying short position in the market had become so large by the late stages of the gold bear market as to pose a serious threat to the financial health of the bullion banks (the big investment banks), and therefore to the financial system as a whole. Consequently, they assert, this led to an effort on the part of these banks, covertly supported by the US authorities, to manipulate and suppress the price of gold. Other conspiracy theorists have also suggested that the US Fed may have been active in attempting to depress the gold price because of the beneficial impact of weak gold for inflation expectations and for sentiment towards the dollar. GATA have alleged, amongst other accusations of market manipulation, that the bailout of hedge fund LTCM in 1998 (see Chapter 3) secretly included a let-out from a 300-tonne short position in gold held by LTCM.

Conspiracy theorists are popularly viewed as being, at best, paranoid and therefore it is not surprising that these allegations of covert collusion in the gold market have been given short shrift in respectable financial circles. However, even though the conspiracy view may be far-fetched it is certainly the case that the gold price has behaved in a very odd fashion on many occasions in recent years, and in ways that cannot easily be explained within the context of normal free market behaviour. For example, after the severe financial problems of Ashanti and Cambior – because of their exposure to gold derivatives – became public knowledge following the huge price spike in gold in September and October 1999, strangely the gold price quickly reversed. Liquidity was restored to the market and by late October much of the gain in the gold price had been given back. At that time one bullion dealer was quoted in the media as follows: 'The market rallied on the Ashanti concerns and now the lower [gold prices] go, the healthier the general marketplace is. Some people who placed bets on that situation are closing them out. People were anticipating a squeeze and they're not getting it.' Another quote was: 'If gold continues to stay at these price levels or lower, then there's less pressure on [Ashanti] and on some other producers and funds to cover their shorts.' Seasoned market players know that completely free markets simply do not behave in this way. If, during an extreme market movement, it becomes known that one or more players are forced buyers or sellers in a quantity that is significant relative to the size of the market, then the market always moves against these players. It does not move so as to allow them comfortably to cover their positions.

It seems evident, therefore, that at least on that occasion there was central bank intervention, unannounced but presumably with the knowledge of some of the big gold market participants. But this is not the same as a conspiracy. Central banks intervene in the currency markets with various objectives in mind, and therefore it may be reasonable to expect them to intervene in the gold market also. Such intervention is generally unwise and unless it is allowed to have monetary policy implications it will also be unsuccessful in the very long term.

During the financial bubble from 1995, though, it seems that central bank activity, coming on top of an extremely long bear market, did destroy what was left of confidence in the gold market and resulted in the gold price being driven down to unreasonably low levels in real terms as miners increased hedging and hedge funds positioned themselves for further declines.

Together with statements, such as that from Bank of England Governor Eddie George, that central bank gold sales were simply a perfectly reasonable portfolio decision, the sales by central banks had the maximum negative impact on gold market sentiment. The continuous fall in the gold price then interacted with the bubble in stock and bond markets to intensify the trends in all the markets. A relevant anecdote is the following quote from early 2000, attributed to a gold importer in India (the world's largest consumer of gold): 'Almost all gold investors have started putting their money in the share market because the returns are almost double that what they get (*sic*) from gold trading.' The result can be illustrated quite simply in Figure 5.4, showing the ratio of the S&P 500 index of the US stock market to the gold price – the value of the US stock market in terms of gold – over the past 130 years. The chart is shown in log terms because the stock market should naturally be expected to out-perform gold quite strongly over time, because gold has not historically provided any real return to investors. Nevertheless, even when viewed in log terms and considered relative to the upward-sloping nature of the long-term trend, the rise in stocks relative to gold over 1995–2000 can be seen to have been completely unprecedented.

The weakness of gold helped encourage further investment in stocks and bonds, feeding back into further weakness in gold. But there were other, more fundamental, feedback effects at work. Weak gold prices encouraged very influential economists such as Wayne Angell, Jude Wanniski, Lawrence Kudlow and others to believe that Fed monetary policy was tight. One (of many) examples of this thinking was a 1999 article written by Brian Wesbury, the chief economist at Griffin, Kubik, Stephens and Thompson, from which the following quote is taken: 'The Fed pays lip service to "new era" high-tech productivity growth, but underestimates its power. Thus it argues that there are too many jobs, that higher wages will cause inflation, and that rising stock prices are bad for the US economy. Yet the best

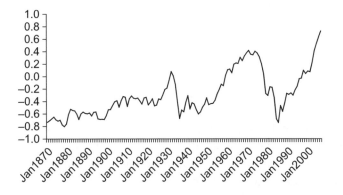

Figure 5.4   Log S&P/gold 1870–2000

thermometers of inflation – commodity prices and gold – are telling us exactly the opposite' ('Repeal Humphrey–Hawkins', *Wall Street Journal*, 22 July 1999). Mr Wesbury argued in his article that weak gold prices were indicating that Fed policy was too tight, a view shared by economists such as Wayne Angell and Lawrence Kudlow. But in reality he was creating a 'straw man' in suggesting the Fed paid no attention to gold and commodities. They almost certainly did pay attention, and in total contradiction to the views of Mr Wesbury and the others, artificially low gold prices probably helped mislead the Fed into thinking that policy was appropriate, when in fact it was excessively loose.

In the markets weak gold prices helped suppress inflationary expectations. They may have played a part in helping depress the prices of other commodities also – which were generally declining from 1995 and particularly weak in 1998 – encouraging speculation against commodities such as oil. The falling gold price also helped boost sentiment towards the dollar, increasingly seen as the long-term replacement for gold as a safe store of value globally. The strength of the dollar, in turn, directly helped to keep down inflation in the US.

The Dollar

In Chapter 3, it was explained that dollar strength was integral to the financial bubble that built up in the US from 1995–96, and was echoed across the rest of the world's financial markets. The huge structural bubble in the US implied an increase in the demand for US money, one manifestation of which was a strong dollar. One conclusion was that the unwinding of the bubble must be associated with severe dollar weakness. The behaviour of the currency and the financial markets as a whole have been inextricably tied together as part of the bubble phenomenon, and the demise of the US markets (particularly the bond market) and the dollar must go together.

In Chapter 2, in a discussion of the enormous imbalances of the US economy, it was suggested that a dollar decline in excess of 30 per cent against other major currencies would be the minimum necessary to bring the US balance of payments on current account back towards balance. In this context the required fall in the dollar must take the form of a real decline, that is a fall in the real exchange rate, or a depreciation that is not offset by higher domestic inflation and therefore makes the economy more competitive. It requires a real exchange rate decline, other things being equal, to boost export competitiveness and to reduce the real purchasing power of consumers, thereby helping to correct the imbalance between savings and investment. The financial bubble was the original cause of the real exchange rate for the dollar becoming too high – because it led to excessive investment relative to savings and drew capital into the US – and its bursting would naturally be expected to lead to a real dollar depreciation. However, to the extent that the financial bubble also artificially stimulated demand for US money holdings, then a purely nominal depreciation of the dollar (that is a fall in the dollar that is associated with higher inflation and therefore does not increase US competitiveness) should also take place as the bubble unwinds. As the asset bubble unwinds, the associated fall in the demand for US money will cause the accumulated monetary excess to be realized in the form of a weaker currency and higher inflation, as already described in Chapter 3.

In short, there will eventually be both an inflationary element and a competitiveness aspect to the decline of the dollar. In the past it was often argued that a 10 per cent fall in the dollar exchange rate tended to increase the US inflation rate by roughly 1 per cent, based on the direct effect on the price indices of higher import prices consequent upon the dollar depreciation. It could be argued, therefore, that the dollar could decline 30–40 per cent, resulting in a higher inflation rate by 3–4 per cent and a gain in competitiveness for the US that would still be around 30 per cent, enough to correct substantially the US external imbalance. However, as discussed in Chapter 3, US money growth has been high for some years, pointing ultimately to a rise in the inflation rate that could well be greater than 3–4 per cent points. If the ultimate rise in the inflation rate were to be greater, obviously an even bigger decline in the dollar would be necessary to bring about the required improvement in US competitiveness.

We cannot know what will be the final result of the collapse of the asset price bubble in terms of the magnitude of the eventual decline in the dollar and rise in the US inflation rate. We do know that monetary economic theory suggests that eventually both a substantial dollar depreciation and a significant rise in the inflation rate must occur. Clearly, both in perception and in reality, when they do occur there will be important links between the two phenomena. In theory they are linked because the exchange rate for the dollar is a measure of the external value of US money while the level of prices provides a measure of the internal value, to which the external value must relate in the long term. However, in the context of the bubble and its bursting there are important feedback mechanisms between the dollar and inflation that go beyond this. During the bubble the strength of the dollar helped keep inflation expectations in the US low. It also helped to suppress the price of gold and other commodities, further reinforcing the tendency to low inflation expectations. As long as inflation expectations remained low then the demand for US financial assets, including money, remained strong, given that this was accommodated by the Fed's loose monetary policy.

As explained previously, strong demand for money helped perpetuate low inflation. These were some of the circularities and feedback effects that characterized and sustained the structural bubble.

Why has the dollar not collapsed as the structural bubble has been unwinding? By the end of 2002, the dollar had fallen from its peaks against the major currencies. But as yet the scale of the decline is small compared both with the magnitude of the appreciation that took place during the bubble and compared with the decline that will ultimately prove necessary to correct the US external imbalance. This has been true even though the bubble has been unwinding for nearly three years. In Chapter 4, it has already been explained that, even though the stock market has fallen so severely, the structural bubble is still very much with us in the form of a giant bubble in the bond market. To the extent that this is so the dollar remains supported. However, there are a number of other factors that have helped support the dollar in the face of the Fed's aggressive monetary easing, and have thereby slowed the process of bubble unwinding. These need to be mentioned because they represent further ways in which governments and central banks around the world have acted to sustain the bubble and forestall the process of correction. They are: (1) the global nature of the asset bubble and foreign central bank reaction to its unwinding; (2) foreign government and central bank support of the dollar; (3) the exceptionally aggressive easing in US fiscal policy.

During 2001 and 2002 the most common reason given by professional money managers for the failure of the dollar to weaken greatly in the face of obvious US economic problems and aggressive US interest rate cuts was the lack of reasonable alternatives to the dollar. The medium-term outlook for the European economies and Japan was argued to be no better than for the US and, worse still, both Europe and Japan were (correctly) seen as beset by structural economic problems that would greatly inhibit long-term economic growth. Furthermore, the authorities in Europe and Japan were perceived as less decisive than those in the US in taking action to boost economic growth.

There are elements of truth in these arguments, but they are misleading to the extent of being ultimately wrong. One element of truth is that a fall in the long-run growth rate (that is the trend growth rate), such as has undoubtedly been experienced by the Eurozone, does tend to weaken the exchange rate in the short-to-medium term. As the trend growth rate is dropping, the prospective return on investment will be falling, encouraging outflows of capital (to areas of the world where the marginal return on investment is higher). This will tend to weaken the currency. However, these outflows of capital will not be permanent, and will not increase indefinitely. The effect of capital movements is to equalize the marginal return on investment – and

therefore the real interest rate – around the world. This is one of the effects
of free flows of capital globally. Once the trend economic growth rate has
stabilized at a new, lower, level, real rates of return and the currency will
also stabilize. Contrary to what seems to be a popular belief, a permanently
lower growth trend for a particular country or area does not mean a permanently weakening currency for that country. Only a persistently higher inflation rate can lead to continuing currency weakness.

Another element of truth revolves around the fact that inflation in
Europe has remained low and Japan continues to be stuck in a deflation.
A collapse of the dollar against the European currencies and the yen
would tend to raise the inflation rate in the US but, other things being
equal, it could tend to lower it in Europe and Japan (because import prices
would be reduced). This makes a dollar collapse difficult to imagine
because it could worsen Japanese deflation and conceivably push
European inflation rates into negative territory. This fact alone could
make the markets reluctant to sell the dollar down too quickly and therefore result in the dollar decline being more drawn out, at least until such
a time as inflation expectations in Europe are seen to be impervious to
the dollar depreciation.

However, the real truth of the 'lack of alternatives to the dollar' view lies
in the global dimension of the bubble and the central bank response to its
unwinding outside the US. The massive structural asset bubble was US-led
but it was ultimately a global phenomenon. Central banks outside the US
also accommodated the financial bubble, and the feedback effects of the
bubble became causal in economic developments in Europe as well as in
the US. The differences have arisen in the authorities' response to the
unwinding of the bubble that has been taking place since 2000. In the US
the response of the Fed and of the government has been extremely aggressive in terms of actions taken to support economic growth. Very aggressive
monetary easing, in particular, has slowed the process of unwinding of the
bubble. In Europe, the Bank of England and the European Central Bank
have also eased monetary policy markedly. However, the degree of ease
has, by any measure, been less than in the US, and therefore the extent of
support for financial markets has been more limited. What this means is
that, at least at this stage, the rate of deflation of the asset bubble has been
at least as fast in Europe as in the US even though the original scale of the
bubble was so much greater in the US. In the short run this is dollar-
supportive, because of the impression that the European economies are
faring no better than the US, and because the dollar is being insulated from
the direct impact of the unwinding of the US asset bubble. In the long run it
merely means that the true 'day of reckoning' for the US asset markets and
economy is being postponed.

The second factor supporting the dollar has been foreign official support for the US currency. The Bank of Japan has intervened in the foreign exchange markets heavily at times, buying dollars and selling yen to prevent the yen from appreciating. But even more important has been the continuous accumulation of foreign reserves by other Asian central banks that manage their currency exchange rates against the dollar. These central banks – by far the most important of which is the Chinese central bank – hold foreign reserves mostly in dollar assets, and they therefore have continuously accumulated dollar holdings while their countries' balance of payments positions have been in surplus. China's balance of payments on trade and current account has been in surplus for the past decade and as China's share of world exports has accelerated, so has its rate of accumulation of foreign reserves, which surpassed US$250 billion in total in 2002, and are rising at an annual rate of about US$70 billion. These reserves are to some extent held in US Treasuries, helping to account for the fact that as much as 40 per cent of the US Treasury market is now held by foreigners. There is obviously a certain symbiosis between China and the US. China's share of US imports has been rising rapidly and China now accounts for a larger share of the US trade deficit – about a fifth – than any other country, having surpassed Japan. So, to some extent, the deficiency of savings relative to investment in the US (which the current account deficit reflects) is mirrored in an excess of savings over investment in China. These excess savings are channelled back into US dollar assets via the Chinese central bank's accumulation of foreign reserves, in a way that is slightly reminiscent of the 'recycling' of petrodollars during the 1970s oil crises. To the extent that the Chinese remain willing to accumulate dollar assets regardless, then this helps to prevent the dollar from falling in the way that would normally have been expected in light of the US's burgeoning current account deficit.

Unfortunately, as with the other forms of official interference in market processes, government and central bank accumulation of dollars cannot permanently prevent the dollar from collapsing to a level that will be necessary to correct US economic imbalances. In the end, the imbalances are simply too large to be sustainable. Bridgewater Associates estimates that by the end of 2002 the US required about 80 per cent of the world's 'free capital' to finance its current account deficit. The gap between US overall foreign liabilities and its foreign assets (that is US net foreign liabilities) is around US$2 trillion, or about 20 per cent of US GDP. Foreign central bank holdings of US dollars are also estimated at about US$2 trillion, and foreign official dollar purchases (that is central bank buying of dollars) are estimated to have totalled over US$120 billion in 2002, financing about a quarter of the US current account deficit. Asia's share of the overall capital flow to the US has risen dramatically since 2000. Unless foreign official support for the dollar continues to increase, the dollar will continue to slide. The risk is that at some point foreign central banks – including the Chinese – will baulk at holding such huge foreign reserves in a depreciating currency and will slow their accumulation of dollars and diversify reserves into other currencies. The withdrawal of official support for the dollar, on which the US currency now depends to such a large extent, would then likely trigger a 'dollar crisis'.

The third – extremely important but less easy to understand – way in which government action has stalled the dollar decline and forestalled the correction of US imbalances is the US government's massive easing of fiscal policy since 2000. The Bush administration's tax and spending measures have accelerated a deterioration of the federal budget from a surplus equivalent to 2.3 per cent of GDP in the first quarter of 2000 (the time of the stock market peak) to a deficit of 1.8 per cent of GDP by the third quarter of 2002, a massive swing of 4 per cent of GDP. This deterioration of the government savings position has been enough to offset the rise in the desired personal savings rate consequent upon the stock market decline (see Chapter 2). The economics of this is that, other things being equal, a fall in desired savings relative to desired investment, in the first instance, is a factor that tends to strengthen the currency. The emergence of a savings deficiency, in this case, at first acts to boost the economy and draw in capital from overseas, strengthening the currency and thereby creating the current account deficit that the savings deficiency implies. In contrast, a rise in the desired savings rate relative to investment (such as has clearly happened since the stock market bubble began to burst) should have the opposite effect, causing the currency to weaken and the current account to improve. However, if the government changes its own savings and investment behaviour, then it can offset this. This is effectively what has happened since the beginning of 2000. By running a sharply increased deficit the US government has cut its own savings (that is government revenues minus government consumption) relative to its investment spending, preventing the economy's overall savings investment imbalance from correcting. While this process is happening it is dollar-supportive, but once a new position of a stable – and higher – deficit has been reached, it will be negative for the dollar. Once again, the actions of the official sector have forestalled the corrective process at the cost of making the problem worse in the long run.

The Forces to Higher Inflation

This chapter has been concerned with explaining why the reasons commonly given for expecting deflation in the global economy are, at best, only factors that help explain temporary falls in the inflation rate, and how official intervention and interference in market processes have prolonged the feedback effects of the structural bubble that have been the important factors keeping inflation low. As the bubble continues to unwind, these feedback effects inevitably go into reverse, ultimately releasing higher inflation. The dollar will fall heavily, gold will rise strongly and inflation expectations will begin to rise, ultimately hitting bond markets. The eventual result of the very loose monetary policies that originally created the financial bubble, and that have been sustained since the bubble began to unwind, must be inflation.

The role of debt in this process has already been addressed. Most economists and commentators seem to see excessive indebtedness as a deflationary threat, but in reality it is a force towards inflation if central banks accommodate to allow for its monetization. In this context, the degree to which consensus opinion has abandoned the money supply as a worthwhile indicator or target, forgetting the lessons of the 1970s, is disturbing. The European Central Bank (ECB) has come under a barrage of criticism for continuing to include a target for broad money supply growth as part of its framework for setting monetary policy. The IMF has been very critical of the ECB, and the Bank for International Settlements (BIS) has also argued that central banks need be less worried about inflation than in the past. The ECB itself has honoured its money supply growth target – of 4.5 per cent annual growth for M3 – more in the breach than in actuality (see Figure 5.5). The ECB and market commentators have been particularly disingenuous in making various excuses for excessively high M3 growth – such as financial market uncertainties and non-resident holdings of M3 boosting the demand for money – while totally ignoring the fact that the introduction of euro notes and coin artificially reduced money supply growth. The reality is that Eurozone M3 growth has been consistently too high to be consistent with the ECB's objective of keeping inflation below 2 per cent.

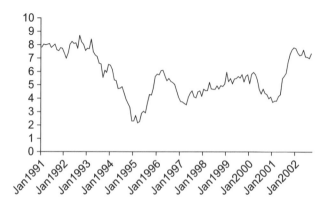

Figure 5.5 Eurozone M3 growth

This is not surprising because the euro construct is itself inflationary in nature. There was not enough convergence between the Eurozone economies prior to the adoption of the euro to allow for inflation to be very similar across the member states. In the absence of the possibility of exchange rate realignments, a Eurozone member economy requiring an adjustment to a greater level of competitiveness would be forced into an unacceptable deflation. To allow for necessary economic adjustments between member economies, in the end the average inflation rate across the whole Eurozone needs to be fairly high. Otherwise, or perhaps as well, the ECB will be forced into loose monetary policies to alleviate financial stresses within the zone. These kinds of factors are already evident in the calls of some economists for the ECB to raise its inflation limit above the current 2 per cent level. Residents of the Eurozone already believe inflation is higher than allowed for in official statistics, as demonstrated by the protests against price increases that took place in some of the Eurozone countries – Italy in particular – in 2002.

In the US, too, any attention paid to money supply growth is widely considered to be anachronistic. In 2000 Congress debated whether to scrap the Humphrey-Hawkins legislation under which the Federal Reserve chairman has to account for his Fed's monetary policy to the Congressional banking committees. As Reuters news agency reported it, 'For some time, there has been a feeling in Congress that Humphrey-Hawkins is outdated because of its focus on the supply of money in the economy, a preoccupation of policymakers in the 1970s and 1980s' ('Mandated Greenspan Accounting to Congress May End', Reuters, 23 February 2000).

The long bear market in commodities, which was accelerated by the effects of the financial bubble in the late 1990s, resulted in capacity cutbacks in commodity production and a lack of investment in new projects. At the same time there was massive excessive investment in the bubble areas of telecommunications, media, technology and financial services. Together with the tendency to oligopoly in some industries that emerged out of 'merger mania', this provides fertile ground for a future inflation. The complacency of the monetary authorities, governments and nearly all economic commentators only serves to make it more likely. But the main reason for expecting inflation is that this is what monetary theory tells us to expect. Inflation is the logical consequence of the long period of excessively loose monetary policies in the western world. Inflation is also the way through which the financial bubble – in both bonds and stocks – can ultimately be deflated without a debt-induced total financial and economic collapse. And inflation – with a corresponding huge decline of the dollar – is the way through which the economic imbalances that beset the world will finally be resolved.

CHAPTER 6

The Institutions' Role in the Mania

Institutional Investment in the Bubble

The previous chapters have sought to demonstrate that the loose monetary policies of central banks and their acquiescence to the wishes of the financial markets, as well as the various interventions of governments, created an environment of easy money, moral hazard and, ultimately, self-reinforcing economic and financial feedback effects. These combined to create the monster of the financial market bubble that dominated the world economy by the end of the 1990s. Yet this cannot be quite the whole story. People had actually to buy the stocks – and the bonds – to push them to the completely outrageous price levels that were ultimately seen. Throughout the history of financial markets there have been very many financial manias, and Charles P. Kindleberger's famous book on *Manias, Panics and Crashes* explains how cycles of extreme speculative euphoria develop. However, modern markets are supposedly dominated by professional investors acting for large institutions, such as pension funds, insurance companies and mutual fund complexes, who might be thought immune from such speculative urges. Are they not supposed to be using very sophisticated methods to value stocks and markets that should steer them away from investments that are becoming clearly overvalued and therefore unable to provide a satisfactory long-term return? And, given their dominant position, should not their actions in doing this help to prevent the markets from moving to too great an extreme?

Unfortunately, by the late stages of the 1980s and 1990s bull market, the institutional investors had become very much part of the process of the mania. It is somewhat ironic that, in the recriminations over the failures of corporate governance seen by many as the main culprit in the bubble fall-out, these very same institutions are thought to provide the solution. As *Financial Times* columnist Tony Jackson has written,

'The drumbeat of shareholder activism, it seems, is getting louder by the day. Companies have gone wrong and must be punished ... The government now has a stated aim "to promote more active engagement by institutional shareholders ... [This] will build stronger companies". Now, hang on a moment. In any list of business failures these days, a top slot must surely go to the savings industry. Its main job of asset allocation has been systematically botched ... Those responsible, it seems, cannot run their own affairs. Why then should they intervene in other industries rather than, say, the other way round?'[15]

In order to understand how the savings industry 'botched its main job of asset allocation' it is necessary to understand the constraints the industry has operated under, and how these constraints interacted with the economic processes that encouraged the financial mania, to create the huge structural bubble. These constraints could be said to boil down ultimately to a lack of faith on the part of pension fund trustees and insurance companies in their fund managers, which results in excessive attention to short-term investment performance and an overly narrow view of risk control. This underlying lack of trust was perhaps itself an inevitable consequence of the long bull market. The vast sums of money that could be earned as markets moved inexorably higher from the early 1980s drew an increasing number of companies into the business of asset management, encouraging greater salaries and bonuses and more and more movement of key personnel. For the trustees and plan sponsors of large pension funds, this lack of stability in their fund management teams, whether in-house or with the asset management companies to which they contracted out the management, inevitably caused a shift in their emphasis to investment 'processes'. The notion that there is an investment 'process' in place can give those with the ultimate responsibility the comfort that their funds are being managed in a consistent way, even if the actual people doing the management change from one month to the next. The pension fund consultants and actuaries, who became increasingly important as advisers to fund trustees from the 1980s onwards, helped drive this emphasis to clearly defined fund management styles and processes. For an asset management company trying to win new pension fund business, it was no longer enough to demonstrate high-quality research and investment ideas. The minutiae of how research and ideas translated into actual portfolios – the 'process' – became the critical element.

Investment processes are discussed later in this chapter. Another aspect of plan sponsors' lack of faith in the abilities of their asset managers has been the emphasis placed by many on comparatively short-term measures of investment performance. Processes are all very well, but from the trustees' point of view they also want to know that the returns on their pension fund assets are satisfactory and will continue to be satisfactory. The question facing trustees, during any difficult period for the investment performance being achieved with their assets, is how much of a period of grace to give their fund managers. Is a period of poor performance just one of those inevitable occasional hiccoughs reflecting difficult financial market conditions or is it a sign of something more fundamentally wrong with the fund management team and the investment approach they are using?

During the long bull market, as various of the growing number of asset managers achieved periods of exceptional performance, the patience of trustees and plan sponsors with under-performing fund managers grew thinner and thinner. Fund managers were increasingly measured on a quarterly basis against their peers managing similar funds and against the relevant stock market indices. In October 1999 the pension fund of Unilever PLC sued Merrill Lynch Mercury Asset Management (MAM), seeking damages of £100 million for under-performance of the pensions assets it had been managing. Shortly after, the manager of the pension fund of UK supermarket chain J. Sainsbury was quoted in the British press when he called for heavy financial penalties for under-performing fund managers, crystallizing the pressures on fund managers for performance at least in line with indices. It became a familiar lament of fund managers that they 'could not afford to be out' of the overvalued technology stocks. Even if a fund manager believed that these stocks were grossly overvalued (which of course they were) he had to hold them in the portfolios he managed because they were appreciating exponentially, and they were in the indices and his competitors had them in their funds. To exclude them meant risking his job.

It is well known that emphasis on short-term investment performance exacerbated the markets' bubble tendencies. But the issue ultimately ran deeper than this because it became a problem of the structure of the investment industry. As the mania ran on and on, investment companies that practised a 'growth investment' style (see below) swept all before them. They attracted more institutional accounts and more retail money into their mutual fund complexes. The result was more and more money committed to growth stocks. Experienced investors used to believe that when most of the market was bullish on a stock or group of stocks, or the whole market even, it must be near the top for that stock or sector or market because 'everyone must already own it, leaving no one left to buy'. The late-1990s mania completely reversed this logic. Everyone being bullish simply meant more of the flow of new investment money being directed into the 'hot' technology, media and telecommunications stocks, as these stocks began to constitute an increasingly large proportion of the indices and of the universes against which the investment funds being run by the fund managers were being measured.

As assets under management grew rapidly with the increasing value of the markets, the more aggressive financial institutions were able to gear up their own balance sheets, taking on debt to acquire other fund management institutions. With the markets, and therefore the fees to be taken from managing funds invested in the financial markets, soaring, the return on investment in the industry of fund management itself was extraordinarily high. Merger and acquisition deals in the asset management industry came one after another over the period 1997–2000. The logic for the deals was usually the notion that asset management companies needed to achieve 'critical mass' to give them the clout to be considered serious contenders in the business of managing large institutional accounts. But the reality was that taking on debt to acquire assets under management looked like a sure-fire way to generate a high return on equity when financial markets seemingly could be relied upon to post strong gains year after year. So the more aggressive financial institutions won out and an increasingly large proportion of managed assets came under the control of the 'growth' managers.

This changing structure of the industry had further implications for the flow of investable funds. Mergers meant a polarization of the industry into very large asset management institutions each managing tens, or hundreds, of billions of dollars and boutique operations, such as the hedge funds, managing a few hundreds of millions. It is not possible for large companies to manage funds in a way that is genuinely active, taking investment views that are significantly different from the consensus of opinion and positions in portfolios that diverge markedly from market index weights. Simple polls of fund managers' views can show that once there are more than about 25 fund managers in a room, the average of their expectations will accord fairly closely with the expectations already discounted in the markets. Large fund management groups, making asset allocation decisions by committee, therefore cannot reach opinions that are very different from market consensus. Instead, the large groups became basically sales and marketing machines, selling a range of 'products' that supposedly met the full range of investor requirements. In the mania, this meant basically selling and promoting the products that were going up, that is 'growth' stock funds.

There were also more subtle consequences of the emergence of the 'mega' managers. If an organization is basically a sales and marketing organization then the way for its employees to get ahead within it is through selling and marketing. Investment research becomes secondary, and only really of benefit to the company if the marketing effort can be leveraged off it. The company is not really 'doing investment' anyway. In this environment the growing number of people being attracted into the industry and succeeding within it in the 1990s were increasingly people whose main talents were in persuasion and presentation, or in succeeding within the corporate environment, not in producing analysis of genuine substance and originality, or indeed in recognizing and understanding such analysis when they saw it. Style won out over substance. The fact that the financial markets seemingly could be relied upon to carry on providing high returns obscured the fact that the quality of most investment thinking was, at bottom, fairly poor, and there was also plenty of charlatan market analysis that too often received attention that it did not deserve.

With regard to style over substance, there was a symbiosis between the investment industry and the financial media, which grew in size and importance along with the financial markets. The media is interested in news events, which by their nature are short-term phenomena. The growing importance of the media, including the televisual media, encouraged a generation of portfolio managers whose main talents lay in a wide knowledge of national and international affairs and in an ability to discuss the economic news background of the day and its supposed influence on markets. This only helped to add to the short-term biases of the largest market participants and to create an environment in which there is a strong degree of agreement about what it is that is driving markets, from which very few professional market participants depart. The emergence of the mega-managers, the declining quality of investment thinking and analysis, and the growing importance of the media combined to create the global investment backdrop that exists today; one in which most of the time there is a strong consensus about the influences on financial markets. This emergence of consensual thinking was an enabling factor behind the financial mania, and will probably now act to make the ensuing bear market in financial assets much more severe than would be necessary purely to re-establish reasonable valuation levels.

On Wall Street, as equity trading commissions came under pressure from greater competition, the *raison d'être* for the burgeoning number of analysts working for the investment banks increasingly came to be the investment banking business they could help win as hundreds of companies were attracted to go public by soaring stock prices. Negative research reports on companies – never exactly common on Wall Street – became even rarer as there was pressure on analysts not to upset investment banking relationships with corporate clients. These conflicts of interest have come out into the open following the high-profile investigations by the New York Attorney General and the US Securities and Exchange Commission. But they were really part of a wider picture of an across-the-board decline in the quality of research, and of investment thought, as the stock market mania became ever more frenzied in the late 1990s.

So, as with so many other influences on the 1990s bull market and its culminating bubble, the bull market interacted with structural factors – in this case the structure of the securities industry itself – to intensify the mania further. Eventually, even most of those plan sponsors who, cognizant of the long-term nature of their liabilities, might have wished for a less short-termist approach to be applied to the management of their assets, were forced to cave in and move their funds to the growth stock managers. Or alternatively they switched to 'passive' management (see below), as asset managers who emphasized traditional concepts of value, or who favoured cash as equities became ever more ludicrously expensive, continued to under-perform. That is, if their fund managers had not already made the shift for them.

The actuarial profession and pension fund consultants did not exactly discourage the excessive emphasis on equities, either. They had looked at the history and concluded that equities can be relied upon to out-perform other asset classes as long as the investor's time horizon is long enough. It is a short step from that view to believing that the investor wants to be in equities with good earnings growth prospects. The view of the pension fund consultants can be summed up by the remarks of one very senior executive of one of the biggest pension fund advisers to a large gathering of asset managers in 1998: 'We already know that equities out-perform over the long-run. All that remains is a job of education; we need to educate savers to invest in equities.' By the end of the 1990s private pension funds in the US had raised their weighting in equities to over 50 per cent of their financial assets from 35–40 per cent at the beginning of the decade. Public pension funds had gone even further, collectively raising their equity weighting to nearly 70 per cent. Insurance companies were even more aggressive in raising their exposure to equities in the late 1990s.

Investment Processes and Growth Investing

Even growth fund managers were supposed to be operating investment processes, however, and the uninitiated would be justified in wondering why these processes did not take the asset managers out of growth stocks, and out of the stock markets as a whole, as they became increasingly overvalued. There are four major elements common to many investment approaches that resulted in asset managers being misled into believing that the degree of overvaluation of individual stocks and the whole stock market was not as great as it actually was. Most investment processes would have shown equities to be overvalued in early 2000, but many fund managers took the view that, in the end, strong earnings growth would make up for that overvaluation and, in the meantime, it would be impossible to time any market 'correction'. The four problems common to most investment processes were:

1. at the individual stock level, valuations and earnings growth prospects were often considered on a relative, not an absolute, basis;

2. at the level of the whole market, the valuations of stocks were (and still are) considered relative to bonds, which were (and are) themselves overvalued;

3. the consideration of prospective earnings (profits) growth for the market, and for the stocks within it, failed to take into account that the appreciation of the stock market was itself responsible for boosting earnings to a significant extent;

4. more sophisticated models of prospective returns from equities often implicitly built the market 'momentum' into the model forecast for the return.

These factors are discussed below.

Considering valuation in relative terms is a common practice in the securities industry. Bond traders think in terms of the spread between the yield on an instrument and the yield on a relevant benchmark. Equity investors consider the yield on equities relative to the yield on bonds. In itself, this type of relative value analysis is not a bad thing – it lies behind the arbitrage between markets that should help keep the various financial assets efficiently priced. However, in a market bubble, the practice of relative valuation is unhelpful if market participants begin to lose sight of the fact that it is relative valuations, and not absolute measures, that they are looking at. With respect to the issue of valuing equities off bonds, this has been discussed at some length in Chapter 4. The conclusion was that, notwithstanding the well-known drawbacks of comparing equity yields (which have the characteristics of a real, or inflation-adjusted, variable) with bond yields (which for conventional bonds are a nominal measure), valuation approaches using bond yields were flawed because they failed to take account of the impact of the bubble on bond markets. Within equity markets themselves strategists often consider measures of stock or sector valuation in terms of premiums or discounts to sector or market averages. This type of practice reached its unfortunate apogee in the internet mania. With internet stocks having no earnings, conventional approaches to valuation were thrown out of the window. Internet, and other TMT, stocks were often being assessed on the basis of revenues, or more esoteric measures, and then valued relative to other similar stocks in the sector. Thus, an internet stock could be described as 'cheap' because its price-to-revenue ratio was lower than that for other similar companies. This approach obviously lent itself to allowing the market to be 'pulled up by its own bootstraps'.

Absolute measures of valuation used by professional analysts or investment strategists generally use earnings (that is profits) data, rather than corporate net asset values or other possible measures, because data is more readily available. Under one of the somewhat more sophisticated approaches to valuing stocks or markets, the analyst estimates an earnings stream for the next few years, using forecasts for earnings growth or the return on investment, then assumes some path over which earnings growth will converge on the historic market average, and then calculates the present value of the resulting stream of future earnings using an estimated cost of capital comprising a risk-free rate and a risk premium. But, however sophisticated, all of these valuation approaches that used earnings, whether explicitly or implicitly (which includes pretty much all that were in use in the bull market), became victim of the fact that earnings had, to a substantial extent, become a function of the financial bubble itself. This issue has already been addressed in this book, but further elaboration is worthwhile, because the failure to understand the vulnerability of corporate earnings to the bursting of the stock market bubble was undoubtedly the biggest mistake made by institutional investors in the late 1990s.

Three years into the global equities bear market, the full degree to which corporate earnings as a whole benefited from the stock mania, and the degree to which they will suffer as the bubble unwinds, has yet to be understood and fully accounted for. Billions of dollars, and of pounds, have been written off as it has become apparent that companies acquired during the 'merger mania' are not worth what was paid for them. The accounts of many companies have been restated to eliminate cases of profits manipulation and dubious accounting practices, common during the technology boom, such as 'round-tripping' (where a company 'sold' a service to another company and in exchange purchased a product or service back in order to inflate artificially the revenues of both companies). The earnings of fund management companies and investment banks have already collapsed, although they will fall further as financial asset prices continue to deflate. But the true cost of excessive issuance of stock options and the under-funding of corporate pension funds are two aspects of the artificial inflation of earnings that have yet to be recognized fully.

Pension funds, in both the US and the UK, are still in many cases using over-optimistic assumptions for investment returns to assess the degree to which they need to top up their funds. In the UK, years of ill-advised pension fund 'contribution holidays' during the 1990s, when stock market returns consistently exceeded prior expectations, have yet to be made up for. In the US, a report in the *Wall Street Journal* in June 1999 had noted that companies were benefiting from a 'pension windfall' that had, amongst many other examples, contributed 8 per cent of General Electric's pre-tax profits in 1998 and as much as 40 per cent of the profit of Northrop Grumman in the first quarter of 1999. This windfall has now gone into reverse. General Motors forecast a substantial hit to 2003 earnings as a result of cutting its assumed annual return on its pension assets from 10 per cent to 9 per cent, which means that the company has to make contributions to its fund out of earnings, to reduce the degree of under-funding. However, even this, reduced, return assumption – which is in line with that being used by most US corporations – is still too high and eventually will have to be cut further, requiring further deductions from profits. This is discussed further in the final section of this chapter. In the UK, at the beginning of 2003 the combined deficit in the pensions accounts of the largest companies has been estimated (by Morgan Stanley and others) at as high as £85 billion. The methods of accounting for pension funds implicitly allow for market volatility and do not require pension fund deficits to be made up immediately, as long as forecasts for investment income and returns suggest that the longer-term position remains viable. Unfortunately, in the UK as in the US, the return assumptions being used will ultimately prove too optimistic, meaning a further large knock to corporate profits to come.

The other legacy of over-optimism towards equities, and financial assets in general, has been the excessive issuance of stock options by companies as a form of compensation. Traditionally, stock options issued to corporate executives and employees were not included in companies' costs, even though, when exercised 'in the money', they reduce earnings per share and dilute the interests of existing shareholders. In November 2002 bull market darling Cisco Systems announced that its fiscal first quarter net income would have been about 60 per cent lower had it accounted for stock options as an expense and that over the prior three fiscal years accounting for options would have put the company into overall loss. During the bull market, between 1993 and 2001, employees of Microsoft realized gains on options totalling a staggering US$46.5 billion, according to the *Financial Times*. In 1998, reportedly, chief executives of the 200 largest US companies on average earned more than US$8 million each from exercising share options and held unrealized options worth US$50 million. These were large sums of money, which executives were receiving as compensation from their companies, and as companies cannot magically create money from nothing, it is self-evident that these sums represented expenses of the companies concerned. Yet they were not accounted for as such.

As the equity bubble has been bursting the pressure has gone on companies to expense stock options grants and a number of US companies have begun to do so. Standard & Poor's has begun to release estimates of 'core earnings' for the S&P 500 stocks, which adjust earnings for, amongst other factors, stock options grants and pensions. On S&P's measure, the stock options and pension adjustments would have subtracted 34 per cent from 2001 earnings for the S&P 500 stocks. However, the adjustments that companies have made to profits for issues of stock options, or in recent years have reported in footnotes to accounts, have tended to be on the conservative side. Employee stock options are hard to value when issued, leaving leeway for companies to underestimate their true cost (and thereby inflate profits) if they choose. Also, as the economic consultants at London-based firm Smithers & Co. – who did much research on the true cost of stock options to US-quoted companies – have argued, only part of the cost of options occurs when they are granted. A 'Full Cost Accounting' approach, favoured by Smithers & Co., would also take into account the fact that the value of options – and therefore the cost to the shareholders of the company in terms of potential dilution – rises with the company share price. On this basis (taking into account the cost of options exercised and the increase in the value of outstanding options due to share price appreciation) Smithers & Co. estimated that profits for the largest US companies on the full cost basis were only 53 per cent of published profits in 1997 and 37 per cent in 1998.[16]

Now that share prices have fallen substantially, some of this cost will disappear as options are rendered worthless. However, it may not all disappear because US companies have a habit of 're-pricing' options to compensate for share price declines. More importantly, if stock options are now not such a good deal for corporate executives because share prices no longer rise year-in, year-out, how are these executives going to be compensated in future? Presumably with 'real money', meaning that the corporate expenses that were previously hidden in the form of unreported options costs will be clear in the profit-and-loss accounts, contributing to poorer reported profits performance in the harsher stock market environment of the future.

As the equity bear market has unfolded, plenty of evidence of profits manipulation and outright fraud during the late 1990s boom has emerged. The most famous cases are of Enron and WorldCom. The willingness of investors to reward extremely high equity valuations to companies apparently able to demonstrate a steadily growing stream of earnings provided an incentive for corporate management to produce a stream of steadily growing earnings. In some cases this encouraged a flexible interpretation of accounting practices or, in one or two instances, outright fraud to achieve this. Yet many – or in fact most – professional investors remained blind to the ways in which the stock market bubble was leading to an artificial inflation of profits in the late 1990s. It was commonly argued that profits were actually being *understated*, explaining high equity valuations. One such argument being made in 1999 was that US corporate profits were being understated because companies were required to expense 'investments' in software and research and development when really these should have been capitalized and depreciated over a period, meaning higher profits in the short term. The fact that arguments such as these, being made by the majority who were still bullish on stock markets in the late 1990s, carried more weight at the time than the evidence of profits manipulation, excessive use of options and revaluations of pension assets and so on, merely showed the mental stretches that investors were only too willing to make to justify their own exposure to equities.

What was it that was driving individual fund managers to feel fairly comfortable with a high exposure to equities, and particularly growth equities, at the height of the mania? Asset allocators – more often asset allocation committees – usually consider valuation and prospective earnings growth, along with indicators of 'liquidity' (see Chapters 3 and 4) as being key variables when deciding on portfolio weightings for different equity markets or equity market sectors. They may also include other economic indicators and market momentum, as well as non-economic factors such as potential political influences. During the bull market, 'quantitative' investment approaches, which used statistical models to combine these various elements, also became increasingly popular amongst the investment community. The reason for the greater popularity of quantitative approaches to asset allocation was, first, that the huge increases in computing power made them feasible and, second, that they seemed to satisfy the desire of pension funds and their consultants for 'process', that is a clearly definable way through which investment ideas, forecasts and assumptions could translate directly into actual portfolios. Assumptions about current earnings and prospective earnings growth for different equity markets, measures of liquidity conditions, interest rates and other factors that had been found to be statistically relevant could be plugged into the model to spew out anticipated returns (over the next period) for different markets or sectors, which could then be used to derive optimal portfolio weightings in each of the markets or sectors. In a typical growth fund manager approach, the required weightings in the various markets or sectors would then be attained by the fund manager investing in the growth stocks in those markets or sectors (that is stocks with a relatively high rate of expected earnings growth).

This sort of approach seems scientific, but in reality the forecasts of 'top down' quantitative stock market models (models that use economic and other macro-data to derive forecasts) tend to be influenced by the existing market trend. It is almost inevitable that, if a trend has been particularly persistent, the statistical parameters of the model will build in that trend and incorporate it, to some extent, in the projections. By early 2000, the US stock market had been in a bull market for the best part of 20 years, the final five of which had seen the S&P 500 provide a total annual return in excess of 20 per cent. As trends go, this was probably the most persistent that has ever been seen in a market. It was almost inevitable that, despite extraordinarily high levels of valuation, most quantitative macro-models would not project strongly negative returns. Most importantly, traditional quantitative models cannot abstract from the feedback effects between the different influences on the markets that are present in a structural bubble, and therefore they cannot project the reversal of these feedback effects when the bubble bursts.

Quantitative macro-models therefore tended to provide a degree of false comfort for fund managers, reassuring them that they would not come to too much harm following their natural inclination to be bullish in a strongly rising market. Perversely, the more sophisticated the model the more likely this was to be true. Highly sophisticated models, incorporating many variables to produce a strong 'fit' (that is that historically appear to explain well the past behaviour of the market), were more likely to be capturing implicitly the well-defined market trend during the bull market. At the same time, because the statistical equations that comprise more sophisticated models require expert statisticians to produce them (generally part of in-house research teams in the fund management houses and the investment banks), they are unfathomable to most fund managers (who, for the most part, are not expert statisticians). This leaves fund managers, in their own minds, tending to fall back for reassurance on old 'rules of thumb' while deriving some residual comfort from the 'black box' models. The rules of thumb during the bull market revolved around earnings growth, market momentum and interest rates. As far as most fund managers were concerned, equity markets were never going to perform poorly for long if earnings growth was going to remain strong, and interest rates were not too high.

Market momentum itself even became a respectable investment criterion during the long bull market and its ultimate mania. The European edition of the *Wall Street Journal* noted this in an article entitled 'US Investors Have Put Faith in Momentum' (15 March 1999). This article considered momentum investing on a broad definition, including earnings momentum (that is buying stocks that are experiencing upward revisions in earnings estimates and strong earnings growth) as well as pure price momentum (that is stocks that have been rising in price). The article referred to work by Richard Bernstein, quantitative strategist at Merrill Lynch, which showed that momentum styles of investing had been easily the most popular amongst fund managers. By the end of the bull market, pure price momentum had become a proven successful investing style. Morgan Stanley Dean Witter strategist Byron Wien discussed this in a piece of research published on 7 February 2000:

'Also, within the last few years, price momentum has become a respected approach to investing. Buying out-of-favour stocks that represent good values and being patient has been punished. The more the momentum approach has worked, the more followers it has attracted. The Ned Davis procedure of buying the top-performing 5 per cent of his 1,900 stock universe and holding these stocks until they drop below the top 10 per cent has beaten the S&P 500 for 60 per cent of the months since 1972.'[17]

This return to momentum investing inevitably grew much stronger towards the end of the mania. In a piece of UK research published on 8 March 2000 by the London-based strategy team at Dresdner Kleinwort Benson, entitled 'Method in the momentum?', the authors noted, 'Relative price momentum has outperformed over the last six months by 35 per cent plus and by 10.8 per cent in February alone ... valuations have not been the real driver for share prices.' Dresdner had previously noted that price momentum as an investment style had out-performed by 11 per cent in 1998, and had been successful in the UK since 1994.

In short, fund managers in early 2000 were working in an environment where previously successful investing styles based around earnings and price momentum continued to work very well and satisfy the need for short-term performance, where many supposedly sophisticated quantitative models were not pointing clearly in a negative direction, and where the tried and tested investment 'rules of thumb' continued to provide reassurance. Unfortunately, as has now become clear, ultimately all investment 'rules of thumb', and also quantitative models, must fail if and when they become widely accepted. The most spectacular failure of this sort has been the failure of stock markets to recover even as interest rates have been slashed. Prior to the equity bear market that began in 2000 most investors believed that three interest rate cuts by the US Fed would herald a market recovery and a new bull market. 'Don't fight the Fed' was the common refrain. In fact, it was inevitable that the bear market, when it eventually arrived, would coincide with falling interest rates. This is because the belief that the Fed would cut rates in the event of a severe market fall was fundamental to the bull market (see Chapter 3). Investors had already priced in the certainty that the Fed would reduce rates if the stock market fell substantially and the notion that such interest rate cuts would rescue the market. This was part of the 'moral hazard' that was a key cause of the mania. If the market was ever going to fall – and the laws of economics said that the market was not going to stay grossly overvalued for ever – then logically it was going to be falling *despite* the fact that interest rates were being cut, and this is indeed what has happened.

Over 1998–2000 professional investors had looked at earnings growth, the strong market momentum and the fact that interest rates, although rising from 1999, were still low, and concluded that it was right to be fully invested.

If they were growth investors – and by the end of the bull market most active fund managers had a growth bias – they were, by definition, investing in growth stocks. Without realizing it they were doubling and tripling up their bet on strong earnings growth and market momentum continuing. The models they were using calculated fair market levels on the basis of the high level of current earnings and the widely held view of strong earnings growth continuing into the future. They also, for the most part, built into projected returns a degree of the strong prior trend of market returns. The fund managers were then using these models to justify heavy weightings in equities, which were then invested in the stocks expected to have particularly high earnings growth. There was a circularity in all of this – an excessive reliance on the belief in strong earnings growth without a recognition of the fact that, to a significant extent, strong earnings growth was itself dependent on a continuation of strong stock market performance. The average fund manager was taking a great deal of risk in his portfolios. But the irony was, at a time when the monitoring and control of risk was supposedly much more scientific than ever before, the sophisticated risk management procedures used by the fund managers did not show up this risk at all. The culprit for this was the modern portfolio management obsession for 'benchmarking'.

Risk Control and Benchmarking

Unilever pension fund's lawsuit against MAM highlighted the obligation upon fund managers in the modern world of portfolio management to control the overall risk of their portfolios, where this risk is defined in terms of the likelihood of the portfolio's return deviating substantially from that of a predetermined 'benchmark'. The benchmark for an equity portfolio is usually a stock market index or a subset of an index. In the case of Unilever, MAM were reportedly alleged to have under-performed the agreed benchmark by 10 percentage points over the course of a year. Obviously, for the fund manager, the risk of such under-performance can be reduced by constructing a portfolio of shares that is much more like the benchmark agreed with the client. If the benchmark is the S&P 500, if the portfolio is built to contain most of the larger stocks in the S&P 500 in the relevant weightings, then the risk of the portfolio's return deviating substantially from the return on the S&P 500 will be small.

In the jargon of portfolio management theory, the risk of a portfolio deviating from its benchmark is described in terms of its 'tracking error', also known as 'active risk'. The tracking error is a percentage figure for the range within which the portfolio's return relative to the benchmark's return should be expected to fall roughly two-thirds of the time. So, for instance, if the tracking error of a portfolio is calculated at 4 per cent, in roughly two out of every three years the portfolio's return should fall within 4 per cent, on either the positive or negative side, of the return earned by an investment in the benchmark. The prospective tracking error of a portfolio can be estimated using a risk model such as the Barra risk model, which calculates tracking errors for portfolios on the basis that the way in which stock prices behave relative to each other in future will be statistically consistent with past behaviour. A Barra model can be used to derive optimal weightings in different equity markets for given tracking errors and given expected returns, which in turn might be derived from the type of quantitative model for expected returns described earlier.

In the late 1990s asset managers became obsessed with tracking errors for their portfolios as the need to minimize the risk of sharply under-performing the benchmarks provided by their institutional clients, the pension funds and the insurance companies, increased for even very short-term horizons. It was common for asset managers to be assessing share holdings in portfolios for signs of under-performance relative to the market on a weekly basis, selling shares that showed signs of such under-performance, while at the same time minimizing differences between their portfolios and the benchmark indices. One thing that pension funds really disliked – as exemplified in the Unilever case – was when their portfolio under-performed the benchmark but other, similar, portfolios managed by the same asset manager for different clients did not. A primary task of heads of investment became to ensure consistency of portfolios across the different portfolio managers in their teams. Consistency, together with low tracking errors, added up in many cases to 'closet benchmarking', that is portfolios that looked rather like the indices they were being measured against.

Indexation reached its extreme in the fashion for 'passive investment', which was the other big winner amongst approaches to equity investment – along with growth investing – in the late 1990s mania. With stock indices performing so strongly and most fund managers having difficulty out-performing them, many institutional investors (and also retail investors, who bought index-tracking funds) took the decision to index their portfolios, that is invest them exactly in line with the composition of the chosen stock market index so that the portfolio performance would be exactly the same as that of the index. This was much cheaper than following an active investment strategy because it required much more limited resources and, as a consequence, the fees charged by managers specializing in passive investment were much lower than those for active management. With key indices such as the S&P 500 and the FTSE 100 appreciating so strongly, it seemed that this approach could not really go wrong. And, anyway, from the point of view of the pension fund or insurance company, what was the point in paying heavily for an active fund manager when the portfolio he would come up with would not differ that much from the benchmark index anyway?

The perspective that the pension funds had at that time can perhaps best be summarized with reference to comments made to the press by the finance director of the BBC in June 1999, regarding a decision to move 10 per cent of the assets of the BBC pension fund into an index-tracker fund: 'Against a general trend of growing interest in trackers, you have to say to yourself "what is the payback for accepting that active management is the right thing to do?" The payback has to be a specific beating of a specific benchmark.' Accordingly, the pension fund was tightening up its performance guidelines for its active managers, requiring them to beat given benchmarks by a pre-agreed amount or face being fired.

Three years into the equity bear market, the world looks very different and it is now only too obvious what was wrong with benchmarking and passive investment. Index funds have been the largest holders of stocks that have 'blown up', such as WorldCom, Enron and Lucent, simply because these stocks were significant constituents of the S&P 500. As long as indices were rising strongly, the rapid growth of money devoted to passive investment, whether explicitly or as a result of 'closet benchmarking' (in total estimated to be growing in excess of 20 per cent annually in the US and UK at the end of the 1990s), intensified the trend for the large companies that comprised the major indices to out-perform the rest of the market. Partly as a result, the 'breadth' of the equity markets (that is the number of stocks in a rising trend relative to those in a falling trend) was deteriorating in all of the major stock markets over roughly the last two years of the bull market. The mania had become increasingly concentrated in large, index, stocks and in the fashionable growth areas. Research by Warburg Dillon Read, published in December 1999, showed that 88 per cent of US equity returns from April 1998 up until that date had come from technology and telecommunications. The corresponding figures for Europe and Japan, at 76 per cent and 53 per cent respectively, were also extremely high. For stocks, such as Cisco and Oracle, that were very large and therefore significant index components and were widely believed to have strong growth stories, as well as being in the 'right' area (technology), the sky was the limit.

The composition of the major stock market indices is adjusted regularly to include new companies that have become large enough (in terms of market capitalization) to be included and to exclude those that have shrunk to the extent of not being significant enough. For the UK FTSE 100, for example, this is a largely mechanical process that occurs with changes made on a quarterly basis, with inclusion criteria based primarily on market capitalizations. Companies that have become large enough in terms of market capitalization, either via growth, merger or acquisition, or simply through share price appreciation, can replace other companies that have become smaller as a result of poor relative performance. The weight of each company in the index reflects its market capitalization. The construction of most of the other widely followed equity indices follows the same type of logic, although notably not the Dow Jones Industrial Average, which has been kept true to its long history with a composition of 30 stocks not weighted by market capitalization, the constituents of which are decided by a committee on a partly judgemental basis.

The fact that indices change – in the case of the FTSE 100 and S&P 500 fairly frequently – as the relative market capitalizations of companies change means that passive investors have to change their portfolios accordingly, otherwise performance will be at risk of moving out of step with the relevant index. During the equity bull market, inevitably the composition of the indices shifted to reflect, in terms of greater weighting, those sectors that had been performing particularly well, and therefore growing in terms of relative market size – specifically the 'growth' areas of technology, media, telecommunications, healthcare and financial services. Research from Morgan Stanley Dean Witter (19 January 2000) showed how the S&P 500 had, at that time, become more of a growth stock index as a result of an unprecedented number of changes in its composition over the prior five years. According to Morgan Stanley, in 1999 alone there were 42 changes in the S&P 500, affecting roughly US$450 billion of market capitalization. Not all of these changes were in the direction of adding 'new economy' stocks and dropping 'old economy' stocks, but many of them were; for instance the additions of Yahoo!, Teradyne, Xilinx, Analog Devices, T.Rowe Price, Global Crossing, Qualcomm, Paine Webber and Network Appliance, and the deletions of Asarco, Cyprus Amax Minerals, Battle Mountain Gold, Browning-Ferris, Laidlaw and Rubbermaid. The result, in simple terms, was that the difference between passive investment management and growth investing was becoming less marked in practice than might have been thought from theory. The indices that were being tracked by the tracker funds were becoming 'growth stock' indices.

There was a further quirk to the way that the indices were constructed, that did even more to squeeze up the prices of fashionable large stocks. This was that the weight of each stock in, for instance, the FTSE 100 was based on the total market value of the company, but often much of the stock would be tied up in the hands of strategic, or long-term, investors. An article in the UK edition of the *Financial Times* in February 1999, written by Hugo Dixon (23 February 1999), pointed to the distortions that were being caused by index-tracking investors. The article noted that FTSE 100 companies such as British Sky Broadcasting, Colt Telecom, Orange and TeleWest had less than half their stock floating freely (that is actually available to investors in practice). With estimates placing the percentage of the FTSE 100 and All-Share index companies owned by passive investors at between 10 and 20 per cent (more for the equivalent indices in the United States), there was therefore a limited amount of equity in companies such as these available for other investors, creating an artificial supply shortage. Worse was to come as the equity mania reached its climax. The takeover of Mannesmann by Vodafone created a company that, at one point, represented 16 per cent of the FTSE 100 index, producing a problem for benchmarked fund managers. As Barry Riley noted in an article in the *Financial Times*, titled the 'Curse of Benchmarking', 'The neutral position for a [fund] manager who does not have a view on a stock is not to ignore it but to own a full weighting ... in the benchmarked world, risk is shifted from managers to clients.'[18]

Some of these issues have subsequently been partially addressed by changes in the way that indices are constructed. But the equity bear market will be the final cure for the 'curse of benchmarking'. During the equity mania, benchmarking and passive investing reinforced the exponential rise of the stock indices by drawing more money into the index stocks. A major piece of research published by Crédit Suisse First Boston on 5 November 1999 entitled 'Stock investor behaviour around the time of index changes' found that in the UK market stocks expected to be newly included in the FTSE 100 index out-performed by an average of 4.75 per cent in the three weeks ahead of the change, 4.4 per cent over the two weeks before, and 3.2 per cent in the week prior to being included in the index. Investing in stocks that were going up seemed to be a sure-fire winner because when they became big enough, in terms of total capitalization, to be included in the major index they would go up even further thanks to the activities of index-tracking investors. However, this cannot really be a good way of investing. Buying stocks that have already risen enough in price for their market capitalization to warrant inclusion in the major index and selling them when they have fallen enough to justify exclusion, much of the time will mean buying high and selling low, the opposite of what good investors are supposed to be doing. In normal market conditions passive investing, and therefore benchmarking to an index, is a losing strategy. It was only the abnormal conditions of the 1990s structural bubble that made it look like a winner.

Pension Fund Investment

During the stock market bubble of 1995–2000, pension funds were entrusting equity fund managers with the management of a substantial part of their assets and giving them performance guidelines that implicitly encouraged the managers to invest a large portion of the portfolios in the stocks that comprised the increasingly growth-oriented major market indices. In truth, in an era when 'growth stock' investing had apparently been successful for so long, most active investors, including the professional asset managers, did not actually need too much encouragement to invest in the tried and tested large growth stocks. The part of the portfolio that was not invested in index stocks more often than not would be invested in the smaller and medium-sized 'growth' stocks. Such an approach could produce investment results that appeared satisfactory relative to the performance of indices and relative to the performance of competitors, who were mostly doing the same thing. Those fund managers that did concentrate on value, as opposed to the promise of huge increases in future earnings that the revolution in technology and communications was supposedly bringing, soon found their performance badly lagging, forcing them to change strategy and to 'go with the flow', or face being fired. Such actions obviously contributed to making the asset bubble even bigger, in an economic and financial environment that had become very conducive to the formation of an asset bubble, given the behaviour of central banks and governments.

The logic of the decision underlying the asset allocation of the pension funds was that heavy investment in equities was not necessarily risky for a pension scheme that was not mature (that is not too great a proportion of scheme members were already retired or approaching retirement). For schemes based on the final salaries of members, the investments needed to be able to keep pace with the potentially growing salaries of the members while in work. This could only be achieved through equity investment, the argument went, because history had proved that equities had out-performed bonds over the long-term. Too great an investment in bonds for a comparatively young scheme would risk locking in a level of return (the fixed yield until maturity of the bonds) that might be inadequate in light of employees' rising salaries. A heavy bond weighting in a pension fund portfolio was thought to be appropriate only for a mature scheme. Then the liabilities of the pension scheme were closer to being fixed (the stream of payments of final salaries for each of the members in retirement) and therefore an investment in bonds with fixed coupons was thought to be more appropriate.

Now stock markets globally have been going down for three years, the logic of this argument does not look quite so good and many corporate pension schemes that have kept with final salary-type arrangements are potentially in trouble, being stuck with an enormous deficit in their assets relative to their commitments to future pension payments. But what should pension schemes have done if they should not have taken such a heavy exposure to equity investments? It has been pointed out by some experts that if pension funds had instead invested most, or all, of their funds in corporate bonds, rather than equity, then companies would have been forced to respond to the consequently relatively high demand for debt securities and the relatively low demand for equity by issuing more bonds to fund themselves rather than equity. This, in turn, would have had the consequence of making corporate balance sheets even more geared, significantly increasing risk, and ultimately leading to a higher level of corporate defaults. In fact, in this environment, corporate bond yields would have tended to be higher, providing higher returns but with more risk. They would have been more like equity, meaning that the risks faced by the pension funds in their investments would not in reality have been any lower.

In this book it has been argued that bonds, particularly government bonds, are likely to prove a very bad investment in the long run. For a pension fund, the problem therefore remains that the fixed, low, return to maturity that can be achieved on conventional government bonds in any of the major markets will prove inadequate to meet pensions liabilities. What could have been done, therefore, to provide securely for the future retirements of the ageing populations of the western economies? If stocks were not the answer – as now seems proven – and neither are bonds, as this book has argued, then where should pension funds have been directing their investments?

The answer, unsatisfactorily, is that this is the wrong question to be asking. The underlying problem is that in western societies populations are ageing and people are living longer, and therefore drawing pensions for longer, while relatively the workforce is potentially set to shrink. This is a 'real' economic problem that cannot be solved through purely financial means, however clever. In western Europe, in particular, without significant net immigration in the future there will be many more people in retirement at any one time relative to the numbers that are in work. The standard of living of pensioners, like everybody else's, depends ultimately not on financial wealth but on the consumption of goods and services for which the wealth has been accumulated. The provision of these goods and services in a future of more people not working relative to those that are working necessarily depends on the greater productivity of those that are in work. In turn, this requires a higher level of real savings to finance the investment required to make this possible. It was an illusion to believe, as so many appeared to in the 1990s, that this could somehow be solved through the miracle of levitating financial asset prices. In this light, the contribution holidays that companies took with respect to their pension funds at that time can be seen to have been a foolish mistake, albeit that in the UK, at least, tax law made it a difficult mistake to avoid. Companies, and individuals also, ought to have been putting aside more in savings out of income. Instead, the rapid rise in their stock market wealth encouraged them to do the opposite, making the underlying problem worse.

Over time the appreciation of stock markets must bear some relation to economic growth rates. Equities enjoy a prospective return to risk but this also implies any specific portfolio having some investments go badly wrong sometimes. As was explained in Chapter 4, if we do not assume any compensation for risk, then in equilibrium the total real return from investing in the global equity markets (including dividend income) might be expected to be in line with the growth rate of the global economy. In the future this is not likely to be higher than in the past and, as argued at various places in this book, is quite likely to be lower. In western Europe, the implication of ageing populations and more retirees is that growth will be lower. Against this background, the assumed nominal annual total returns from equities of 8, 9 or even 10 per cent that pension funds in both the US and UK have been using are inconsistent with the widely held belief that inflation will remain very low (a belief that has been fully reflected in bond markets).

Actuaries would argue that the historic real (that is, inflation-adjusted) total annual returns achieved on US and UK equities of around 6.5 per cent (see Chapter 4) justify a prospective return assumption from equities of 8.5–9.5 per cent, assuming 2.0–3.0 per cent inflation annually. The problem with this view (apart from the fact that bond markets in the western economies are discounting a long-term annualized rate of inflation of more like 1 per cent) is that 6.5 per cent cannot be assumed as a reasonable estimate of the prospective real return from equities, except over the ultra-long term, or unless the prospective price–earnings ratio for equity markets is in line with the long-term historic average of around 15–16. Otherwise, the best basis for forecasting the prospective return on global equities (as implied in Chapter 4) is to use the inverse of the price–earnings ratio, that is, the earnings yield on global equities. At the end of 2002 this earnings yield will, at best, probably prove to be closer to 5 per cent than 6.5 per cent, bearing in mind the arguments made about prospective US earnings in Chapter 4.

With a prospective long-term real return of, at best, 5 per cent, global equities could only provide a nominal return of 9 per cent annually if inflation in the major economies is to be at least 4 per cent annually. It has been argued in the previous chapter that 4 per cent or higher annual inflation is quite likely, even probable. Much higher inflation will make higher nominal returns from equities achievable in the long-run – albeit not the same sorts of equities that performed well in the 1990s – but in the short-to-medium run (that is, over the next one to five years) it will mean disaster for bond investments, which must have negative consequences also for equities. Equities are likely to become seriously undervalued, at which point they will genuinely promise high future returns. This is a phenomenon that has so far yet to be seen in the first three years of this bear market.

Pension funds and their fund managers, as well as other investors, should have been assuming much lower prospective returns from equities than they were during the bubble. Contribution rates to pension funds, and other savings schemes, should have accordingly been maintained at a higher level than they were. Pension funds should also have been measuring fund manager performance relative to benchmarks that reflected the structure of their liabilities and not the stock market indices. If all pension funds and other institutional investors had behaved like this would it have prevented the stock market bubble occurring? Probably not entirely, because as this book has sought to explain, the stock market bubble was created by a con-fluence of elements – including the actions of central banks and govern-ments and changes in the structure of the world economy, as well as the behaviour of institutional investors and the financial community – that all came together to create the bubble and the self-reinforcing feedback effects that caused it ultimately to become so huge. Nevertheless, different behav-iour from key parts of the investment industry would obviously have helped a great deal and reduced the financial mess that is now left as a legacy of the mania.

Going forward, there is already evidence of change in the parameters that the various investment institutions are setting themselves, in the growth of hedge funds and new investment fashions, such as the fashion for 'market neutral' or 'alpha' funds. In investment jargon 'alpha' represents the return on a stock (or portfolio) that is specific to that stock (or portfolio), whereas 'beta' represents the element of the return that is attributable to the move-ment of the whole stock market. The concept of 'market neutral' investment funds fits with the idea that any equity portfolio can be considered as com-prising an investment in the stock market index plus a portfolio that repre-sents the 'active' bets that are assumed by the fund manager, in the form of the deviations from index weights of the individual stock holdings. On this approach, the implicit index investment is best managed via a tracker fund. A pure market neutral equity fund, on the other hand, should have no corre-lation with the behaviour of the index, and its performance should therefore rely purely on the fund manager's stock-picking ability.

'Alpha' funds are all very well, but they are seemingly designed for bear market conditions (albeit that fund managers applying market neutral strate-gies would probably disagree) in that the funds have to take short positions as well as long to eliminate exposure to the stock market as a whole. A pos-sible strategy is for the fund managers to buy stocks they believe will out-perform and short those that they believe will under-perform. Alternatively, they could use derivatives to eliminate exposure to the index. Either way, if market neutral strategies started to become too popular in the bear market, the increasing number of short positions in index stocks or in the index would only help to exacerbate the decline of the market averages, just as the fashion for indexation helped to intensify the equity mania.

The huge increase in the number and variety of derivative instruments and the enormous increase in computing power that has become available to professional investors has made ever-more sophisticated and complex investment strategies possible. Concepts such as 'portable alpha' allow for the ability to out-perform in one market to be transferred to another market through the use of financial derivatives. Yet such financial sophistication often obscures some basic principles, which the laws of economics dictate must remain unchanged. They are that, in aggregate, over time stocks as a whole can only provide a real return that is warranted by the achievable long-term performance of the real economy, and the average of investors' portfolios must reflect this real return. Beyond that, the out-performance of some investors must be mirrored by the under-performance of others.

The 'old-fashioned' approach to investment is to make use of sound analysis to discern possible macro-trends and to identify individual stocks that have strong prospects given the macro-background expected, and in which genuine value resides. This at least has the merit of helping savings to be directed to those areas of the economy where they are expected to be of most use and thus helps to make the allocation of resources in the economy more efficient. Even if practised by all investors, at the margin, this should help to raise the economy's growth potential and therefore, to some extent, benefit all investors. This not only suggests that, over time, the 'old-fashioned' approach to investment is superior, and therefore should be the most successful strategy, but it also casts doubt on the true value of strategies that rely too heavily on 'financial engineering' of various forms. One lesson from the past 20 years is that when specific forms of financial engineering become too widely practised – whether it be 'zaitech' in Japan in the late 1980s bubble (in particular the practice of companies raising cheap funds to invest in the stock market) or 'portfolio insurance' ahead of the 1987 global stock market crash – such techniques ultimately tend to be self-destructive. The lesson from the great investors is that, over time, and even though it does not work every time, there is no real substitute for sound analysis, good judgement and realistic expectations.

It is possible that the current bear market will see a swift return to more 'old-fashioned', fundamental approaches to investing. However, to hope for this would be to underestimate the likely effect of the continuing unwinding of the financial bubble on 'real values' in the economy, a subject returned to in the concluding chapter of this book. It is just as likely that new forms of financial engineering geared more to a bear market environment will become more prevalent, exacerbating the financial markets' decline.

CHAPTER 7

Conclusion: What does the Future Hold?

The Legacy of the Bubble

Three years after the US stock market made its final huge peak, there is a fairly widespread belief that most of the worst of the fallout from the giant bubble has been seen. Various individuals, groups and companies have been singled out for blame for misconduct; cynically bullish internet and telecommunications analysts such as Merrill Lynch's Henry Blodget and Salomon Smith Barney's Jack Grubman, dishonest corporate executives such as Enron's Kenneth Lay and Jeffrey Skilling and WorldCom's Bernie Ebbers, untruthful accountants such as those at Arthur Andersen. In the popular opinion these are the people whose fault it all was and now they have been found out, and appropriate remedies put in place, it cannot be long before it is 'business as usual'. Some commentators perceive deeper issues, but along the same lines, pointing to a failure of the whole 'Anglo-American' approach to corporate governance. On this view, the 'old-fashioned' system of management accountability to a board of directors who represent the interests of shareholders is no longer viable in a 'globalized' world where technology rules, information is more important than capital equipment and most of the value of a company resides in the skills of its workforce and the recognition of its brand. This, it is argued, is necessarily the world of vast grants of stock options to senior employees and countless ways for managements to manipulate profits to satisfy the very short-term interests of stockholders.

To this author, there is not much wrong in principle with Anglo-American 'capitalism', taken to mean an economic system in which businesses compete in free markets with the objective of maximizing profits for their shareholders or owners. The problem is rather with the creation and maintenance of a background of monetary and fiscal stability. In fiat money systems central banks operate monopolies over the provision of legal tender money. Monopolies violate the principles of free markets and therefore it is crucial that this monopoly power – particularly given the critical importance of money – is exercised very wisely. The problem in the 1990s was that central banks, notwithstanding their good intentions, did not act particularly wisely. They maintained excessively loose monetary policies and interfered in markets, collectively with governments, in ways which, taken together, created a serious moral hazard that perpetuated the bubble environment. Many of the perceived problems – such as the short-termism of holders of employee stock options or the dissociation between corporate profitability and stock price performance which some blame for failures of corporate control – were products of this environment rather than causes of the bubble and its collapse.

Unfortunately, as this book has sought to explain, the story of the greatest financial bubble of all time is not over, not by a long way. As the bubble continues to unwind – as stock markets remain weak, as the dollar continues to decline, and finally as inflation eventually rises and bond markets fall – there will be much greater distress than has so far been suffered and, inevitably, further recriminations. The 'capitalist' system will come under more pressure, both from those interests that have never liked it, and from others who, misguidedly, believe that the free market system itself is indeed flawed. If these pressures lead to much more government regulation, or major intervention and wholesale changes to the system of corporate governance, then the likely result will be to cement the trend to lower long-term economic growth in the world. Ageing populations in western Europe, the preponderance of red tape and bureaucracy, high tax burdens and the economic costs imposed by the growth of the 'compensation culture' in increasingly litigious western societies already pose enough of a threat to long-term economic growth rates without these added problems. It will be easier than most realize for the global economy to take a step back to the more stagflationary environment that was familiar in the 1970s.

The Likelihood of an Inflationary Adjustment

During the inflationary boom in the UK economy in the late 1980s, the then UK Chancellor of the Exchequer (Finance Minister) Nigel Lawson argued that there was no need for concern about the UK's burgeoning deficit on the current account of its balance of payments because this would be 'self-correcting'. When the balance of payments did eventually 'self-correct' it was through a collapse of the pound out of the Exchange Rate Mechanism of the European Monetary System, amidst much accompanying turmoil in the UK's financial markets. For investors, economic imbalances that are self-correcting are the most dangerous because the process of correction, once it starts, is difficult if not impossible for the authorities to halt, and it can happen very viciously, with dramatic consequences for financial markets.

The process of correction ongoing in the US and global economy since 2000 has, to date, not been of the vicious, sudden, type albeit that the loss of financial wealth has been huge. It has been a drawn-out, and ultimately much more painful, affair because the asset bubble that has been correcting has been a structural, as much as a cyclical, phenomenon. However, the imbalances in the US economy – such as the current account deficit –also have a cyclical element, meaning that a much more vicious phase of the economic and financial adjustment certainly cannot be ruled out. This would take the form of a dollar collapse, as discussed later in this chapter.

The fact that the financial bubble was structural, and therefore has so far been unwinding over an extended period of time while the financial authorities do their best to prop things up, has tended to obscure the nature of the correction that is taking place. Consumer spending in the US, and also in the UK, has remained fairly resilient. In the minds of many observers this fact seems to have suggested that the effects of the bubble on economic behaviour were not as pervasive as might have been feared and, therefore, that the period of 'working off' the bubble excesses may not be too painful. Sadly, this is likely to prove an erroneous diagnosis. Consumer resilience really reflects the fact that the financial bubble so far has not fully burst, a point that has been examined in this book.

Aggressive monetary easing has forestalled a proper correction of the savings rate. It has also supported another aspect of the bubble economy: namely, an excessively high level of house prices, particularly in the main centres in the US and UK. In the UK house prices in real terms have again moved well above the long-run trend given by the growth of GDP and real incomes, as they did at the end of the 1980s. In the US, the National Association of Realtors has estimated that the median value of a single-family home rose around 50 per cent in the decade of the 1990s. Rising home values and low interest rates have encouraged consumers into finance spending through home equity withdrawal, including methods such as 'cash out' refinancing. Notwithstanding low interest rates, this increasing indebtedness does not make sense if inflation is going to remain very low. No inflation would mean no, or very little, house price inflation in the long term, meaning that consumers who engage in mortgage equity withdrawal would be spending future housing wealth. Paradoxically, however, because in the end inflation is likely to emerge to bail out the economy's debtors, those who are taking this course will not bear the full cost of their actions. It is the savers, who have been lending at unrealistically low interest rates, who are likely to be the big losers.

During the unwinding of the bubble, the effects of unwinding might be expected to cascade down through the asset markets and the economy. First the stock market goes down, leading to some weakening in consumer

and investment spending. Corporate profits fall away. Stock prices fall
further and spending weakens further, resulting in rising unemployment.
House prices soften, further pinching the consumer. However, the Fed and
the other central banks have stepped into this process and, for the time being,
prevented the cascade effect from gaining momentum. In doing so, they
have inflated further the bubble in the bond markets and supported the housing market. Ultimately they will not be able to prevent the process of the
unwinding of the bubble from completing, because the economic imbalances that are associated with it are unsustainable, as discussed previously.
On the contrary, there is a risk that their actions in effectively sustaining the
bubble, and therefore the accompanying imbalances, will in the end back-
fire and increase the likelihood of a particularly severe final financial and
economic adjustment.

So far, the aggressiveness of central bank action, together with the structural nature of the bubble, has meant that the reversion of equities markets
(in particular the US market) to fair value levels has been a somewhat less
vicious, but more prolonged, process than it otherwise might have been.
Unfortunately, there is little evidence to suggest that this process is over.
As explained in Chapter 4, a longer-term perspective of valuation suggests
that US equities remain overvalued. More tellingly, they remain above the
levels from which they entered the phase of financial mania, in 1995–96.
The acceleration in stock prices, as shown again in Figure 7.1, began from
that time. This was also the time that other key financial relationships either
began to diverge sharply from previous trends or began to break down completely. This is true, for instance, of the relationship between global industrial production growth and real bond yields, charted in Chapter 2, and also
of the ratio of stock prices to gold prices illustrated in Chapter 5. The stock
price–gold price ratio is shown again, in Figure 7.2, over a shorter time

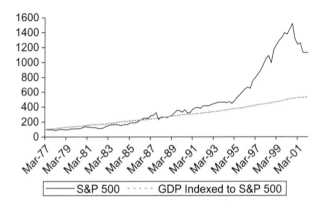

Figure 7.1   S&P 500 and nominal GDP indexed

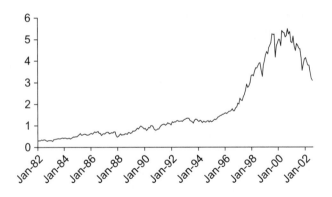

Figure 7.2 S&P 500 relative to gold

frame that shows quite clearly the departure from the previous trend that began from 1996.

The breakdown of the previous trends in, and relationships between, these economic and financial variables reflected the workings of the feedback effects of the bubble that have been discussed in this book. Alan Greenspan made his famous remark about irrational exuberance in December 1996. He was almost certainly right to worry about the possibility that the stock market was becoming irrational at that time, because the acceleration of stock prices and the associated breakdown of other financial relationships were already evident. The Dow Jones Industrial Average was trading at around 6,400 then. By late 2002 the Dow was trading above 8,000 having held above the 7,000 level. A stock market bottom at this level would contravene one of the normal 'rules' of asset bubbles, which is that all of the bubble rise in asset prices is given back when the bubble bursts. Apart from being common sense, this 'rule' has a sound basis in economics, given the economic distortions that the bubble produces. The economic purpose of financial markets is to help allocate the economy's resources efficiently. If the financial markets become irrational, then clearly they are not fulfilling this function. If this irrationality extends to becoming part of a process that has a structural impact on the economy, via the creation of feedback effects, then the distortional effect is even greater. As the process goes into reverse it is hard to see why the markets should stabilize at a higher level than from where the process began, given that the economy's resources have been misallocated in the meantime.

An exception to this could occur if the central bank presides over the creation of significant inflation in the economy. Stock prices, and stock indices, are measured in money terms and therefore, other things being equal, will tend to be higher in the long run if price levels are higher. If inflation is substantial then stock prices could stabilize at a level higher than that at which the bubble began, notwithstanding that a rise in inflation, in the first instance, has negative implications for equity valuations. The principle here can be illustrated very simply with the help of the chart shown in Figure 7.1. During the bubble, stock prices rose exponentially. In doing so, they diverged far from the prices (and values) of the underlying assets, and goods and services, from which are derived the profits streams that supposedly underpin the fundamental value of equities. The chart illustrates this by comparing the S&P 500 index with money GDP for the US, where the GDP data is indexed to start at the same level as the S&P 500 (around 100) in 1977. The point of this chart is not to suggest a 'downside target' for the S&P 500. The chart is comparing the capital value only of a stock index with nominal GDP. It is not necessarily the case that these two series should rise together over time and therefore it is not inevitable that the two lines on the chart will exactly converge again. However, the chart does suggest that the bubble period saw a huge divergence between stock prices and the underlying economy develop, and it seems unlikely that enough of this divergence has been retraced by the end of 2002. The 'gap' can be closed in one of two ways: either via further declines in stock prices; or through an inflation of nominal GDP – or more probably, both.

Those who do not believe that inflation is possible surely have to believe that western stock markets will fall much further than late 2002 levels. A mere return of the S&P 500 index to the 'early bubble' days of late 1995 would see another 30 per cent off this index, and this should be expected to be a very minimum estimate of the likely further decline in an environment in which there is no inflation to 'help out' nominal asset values. Unhappily, even with inflation, the outlook for equities in the medium term will not be rosy either. In fact, investors are used to the idea of an inflationary economic environment being a negative one for equities. Higher inflation would pose particular problems for equities in current circumstances because, as discussed in Chapter 4, it would be occurring against a background in which government bonds are overvalued even on the assumption of very low future inflation, let alone high inflation. Not only would bond yields need to rise to compensate for higher inflation (meaning lower bond prices), but real yields would also rise from the unreasonably low levels that have been a product of the bubble and post-bubble period. Initially, rising long-term interest rates would inevitably be negative for stocks even though they would signal the likelihood of somewhat higher nominal earnings for companies. The arguments that were made for equities in 2002 – that equities are 'cheap' because dividend and earnings yields on stocks are historically high relative to the yields on bonds – would prove to be wrong because of the increase in bond yields. The 'yield ratio' or 'yield gap' would rise from its current historically low level, but because of rising bond yields and not falling equity yields.

It has been a key theme of this book that substantial inflation is ultimately inevitable, as a critical ingredient of the process that will eventually unwind the bubble while correcting the underlying economic imbalances that the bubble produced. Inflation is the logical outcome of the excessively loose central bank monetary policies that originally encouraged the asset bubble, and in the post-bubble environment have been implemented to forestall the process of its correction. Inflation will help reduce the real burden of indebtedness that has also been a legacy of the bubble era. And inflation and, eventually, higher nominal interest rates, in conjunction with a steep fall in the US dollar, will correct the imbalance between savings and investment in the US (and the similar, lesser, imbalance in the UK).

The vast majority of economists and financial commentators would not take seriously the notion that inflation is a looming threat. The arguments here have been discussed at length in Chapter 5. However, those who doubt that significant inflation is now possible in the western industrialized economies need to ask themselves how the economic and financial adjustment required by the US economy, in particular, is going to take place. All the evidence suggests that there has been a financial bubble, which has not fully unwound, and that huge imbalances in the global economy have been associated with this financial bubble. Inflation provides a 'solution' to the imbalances in that it would tend to lead to higher savings rates in the US (and the UK), with higher nominal interest rates, and it would reduce the real burden of indebtedness that has been a legacy of the bubble era.

In this context, it is worthwhile to consider again the relationship between US stock prices and the gold price, discussed in Chapter 5. Figure 7.2 shows the ratio of the S&P 500 to the gold price over a shorter time frame than the chart shown in Chapter 5 (Figure 5.4). The chart is certainly suggestive of a bubble having developed from 1995 onwards, which is now in the process of reversing. The alternative interpretation, which is that there was a fundamental shift in the relationship from 1995 onwards (but with some 'overshooting'), is hard to sustain given what we now know about subsequent financial and economic developments. If we accept the bubble interpretation, it implies that there is still a very substantial further correction to take place in this ratio. Is this more likely to occur via a further large drop in the S&P 500 or, at least in part, as a result of some rise in the gold price? If the latter, it suggests a more inflationary environment.

In Chapter 3 it was argued that monetary policies in the western economies had already been loose enough for long enough to imply a significantly higher rate of inflation in future. There may well be room for debate about this. However, for long-term investors this debate may be beside the point. The really crucial issue is whether or not the financial developments from 1995 onwards have constituted a huge bubble or whether, in fact, there has been a 'paradigm shift' that justifies different financial and economic relationships – between real interest rates and growth, gold and stocks, and so on – from those that existed in the past. If it is a structural bubble (as has been argued in this book) then the unwinding process is not complete. It does not seem likely that the completion of the process will be allowed to happen through further large falls in stock prices. If central banks have not already eased enough to bring about higher inflation, ultimately they will do so.

Stock markets falling a lot further would pose a risk of cumulative financial collapse. Already, the long 'free lunch' that was allowed for by the bull market in financial assets during the 1980s and 1990s is having to be paid for. Continuously rising markets allowed companies to take pension fund 'contributions holidays', and directly boosted corporate earnings in the ways discussed in previous chapters. Pension funds in both the US and the UK used overly optimistic actuarial assumptions for future returns from equities to value their assets relative to their pensions liabilities. They are still doing this to some extent. Insurance companies, similarly, face solvency pressures if stock markets continue to decline. As for the investment banks, financial viability is critically dependent on the level of financial markets and the volume of trading. As the market has slumped, the number of mergers and acquisitions has also tumbled. The bull market obscured a lack of genuine savings in the western economies, particularly in the US and the UK, and the bear market is exposing this. If stock markets fell much further there would be obvious serious risks to the whole financial system.

Central banks can be relied upon to do their utmost to prevent such a scenario from developing. In these circumstances even greater monetary ease would be expected. Widespread complacency with regard to the risks of excessive monetary expansion and inflation only serve to make this more likely. Respected commentators such as the *Financial Times* have been more critical of the European Central Bank, for being the only central bank to pay any attention to money and credit growth, than they have been of the Fed and other central banks that have ignored high rates of money growth. A report in the *Financial Times* in December 2001 noted, 'Wim Duisenberg, ECB president, is seen in London as a supporter of the status quo and a believer in sustaining the legacies of the Bundesbank, such as close monitoring of the money supply. When he is replaced ... it is hoped in London that the reform of the ECB will gain fresh impetus.'[19] This type of sentiment creates an ideal economic climate for policies that create inflation to eat away at the 'wealth' accumulated during the bubble. We can be sure that initial increases in inflation will be attributed to 'temporary' factors, such as rising commodity prices because of 'geo-political uncertainty' or temporary supply disruptions.

Ultimately, the bubble-created 'wealth' must be eroded because it was not 'real' in the first place. True wealth is represented by investment in real assets that produce the flow of goods and services into which financial wealth will ultimately be converted. Inflation reduces the value of the financial wealth relative to the real, and achieves by stealth what would otherwise occur via a much greater collapse of financial asset prices. But even this will be very far from painless for the pension funds and insurance companies. Many of these institutions have cut back on equity holdings and increased investments in government bonds, which are hugely overvalued if inflation rises at all. Even a relatively modest rise in inflation expectations would see the capital values of government bonds in the major markets hit quite hard, and persistent inflation would mean that the investments made by the institutions at very low yields over the past few years would ultimately not be sufficient to meet future liabilities.

In fact, even the inflationary outcome is fraught with the risk of a more vicious financial adjustment, because of the greater constraints that there would then be upon the actions of the Federal Reserve. The position of the Fed has been a little like that of an engineer who is tasked with trying to maintain the water pressure behind a dam that is springing leaks. The engineer keeps pumping in the 'liquidity' to maintain the pressure behind the dam. Unfortunately he does not do anything to solve the basic problem that the dam is structurally unsound. The most sensible approach would be to accept a reduction in pressure while trying to repair the structure fundamentally. The risk assumed by continuing to pump in 'liquidity' is that the pressure will be maintained for a while – and may even increase – but in the end the dam will blow apart completely.

If this is to be the outcome then it would imply roughly the following sequence of events occurring at some stage: the dollar collapsing, the inflation rate jumping in the US, US bond yields jumping and spreads relative to the rest of the world widening sharply, and the stock market falling further. In this eventuality the Fed will not be in a position to ease monetary policy even more to support markets. To do so at that point would only accelerate the decline of the dollar and make matters worse. The burden will be placed on the key central banks in the rest of the world to come to the dollar's rescue by easing aggressively further. In this way the inflation that has been generated by US policies, in particular, will be spread to the rest of the western world. Fears of inflation will not inhibit the non-US central banks from easing initially, particularly as most economists will (incorrectly) argue that the strengthening of the non-US currencies is a disinflationary, or deflationary, force for their economies.

Eventually, this type of inflationary adjustment would pave the way for a more balanced, albeit relatively subdued, economic recovery. It would place great stresses on the global financial system, but in contrast to a non-inflationary, or deflationary, adjustment at least it provides an eventual way out, via the correction of the imbalances in the global economy. The risk of a very serious global financial crisis is still extremely high, however. The modern financial system of globalized markets, with its huge flows of capital across borders and edifice of financial instruments built on top of each other, has emerged over the period of 'disinflation' and low inflation over the past 20 years. It has never properly been tested by a serious swing to a more inflationary psychology, which would be likely to take the form of a 'discontinuity'. If we think back to the 'ants model' of Paul Ormerod (see Chapter 1), the risk is of the 'ants' swinging suddenly from the 'disinflationary' direction to the 'inflationary' direction. Such a discontinuity in the inflation 'regime' would severely test, probably to destruction, the now enormous financial derivatives markets, and not merely the interest rate derivatives markets, taking financial institutions down with them.

The Lessons for Investors

The descriptions of the 1920s and 1930s boom and bust in the financial literature of that time make very interesting reading today because of the very obvious parallels with the financial history of the past decade. The introduction to Graham and Dodd's classic 1934 book *Security Analysis*, written in the aftermath of the 1925–33 stock market bubble and bust, includes a section discussing 'Lowered Standards of Investment Banking Houses' (p.9). This describes how, during the 1928–29 mania, there was a 'wholesale and disastrous' relaxation of standards, which manifested in a surge of new share offerings of dubious merit, aided by 'questionable methods of presenting the facts to the public'. In a passage on the speculative tendencies of human nature (p.11), Graham and Dodd discuss how the culminating phase of the stock market bubble lasted for years, rather than months, as share valuations in the 'new era' were increasingly rationalized with reference to intangible factors such as goodwill, management and 'expected earning power'. It is all very familiar to investors who have lived through the 1990s.

The following passage from *Security Analysis* is particularly apposite in the current context:

'The advance of security analysis proceeded uninterruptedly until about 1927, covering a long period in which increasing attention was paid on all sides to financial reports and statistical data. But the "new era" commencing in 1927 involved at bottom the abandonment of the analytical approach;

and while emphasis was still seemingly placed on facts and figures, these were manipulated by a sort of pseudo-analysis to support the delusions of the period. The market collapse in October 1929 was no surprise to such analysts as had kept their heads, but the extent of the business collapse which later developed, with its devastating effects on established earning power, again threw their calculations out of gear. Hence the ultimate result was that serious analysis suffered a double discrediting: the first – prior to the crash – due to the persistence of imaginary values, and the second – after the crash – due to the disappearance of real values.'[20]

The lesson for now is in the danger of underestimating the destruction of 'real values' brought about by the bubble and its collapse, which can wrong-foot even sound and experienced analysts. In fact in a bubble, it can be the 'gullible' investors who come out on top, because they are 'sucked in' to the bubble at an early enough stage, while more hard-headed investors stay out of the market during the mania, but then make the mistake of buying in when they believe the market has become 'cheap'. Equity investors should remember this whenever those respected market strategists who had been sceptics during the mania pronounce that the time is now right to re-enter the market.

The key is to remember that asset bubbles do not create wealth; they destroy it, as alluded to by Graham and Dodd. But they also redistribute wealth, in a way that concentrates it more greatly. In a normally functioning economy, economic growth means that everyone can become better off over time. Just because one group of people may become vastly more wealthy does not mean that others must become poorer. However, in an asset bubble, with pyramid scheme characteristics, as with a simple chain-letter, the huge gains that some walk away with (usually those that were earlier in the scheme) must be at the expense of others. An investigation by journalists at the *Financial Times* ('Survivors who laughed all the way to the bank', 31 July 2002) revealed that top executives at the 25 largest US companies to have gone bankrupt in the post-bubble period earned a total remuneration of US$3.3 billion over the three-year period 1999–2001. Gary Winnick of Global Crossing, who alone earned US$512 million, heads this list. But even these figures are just the tip of the iceberg. There are the countless other companies at which value has been destroyed. There are the vast sums earned collectively by investment bankers and other financial executives over the bubble period, and still being earned, particularly from the bond markets. Some of those who have acquired this wealth may lose it all again, but most will not. As the financial and economic corrective process goes on, and the 'disappearance of real value' becomes evident, the key to financial survival is to avoid, as far as possible, being one of those who ends up financing the real wealth gains of the corporate executives and investment bankers who gained so much from the bubble.

The most important conclusion of this book is that the crystallization of the loss of real value will eventually take place as much through inflation as through further declines in financial values, although these will occur also. The most obvious implication is that bonds, in the end, will not be a 'safe haven'. On the contrary, they are likely to prove an easy way to lose a lot of money, in particular because central banks will be powerless to protect bond markets that are placed under pressure from rising inflation. Injecting more liquidity into the financial system – the standard way in which central banks have 'underwritten' equity markets – will not work, because it will only threaten to make inflation pressures worse. The structure of the whole bond market – both government and corporate – is potentially much more vulnerable than it was at the time of the last great bond bear market, in the 1970s. The markets are so much more vast, and there is now a huge market in financial derivatives, a large proportion of which are traded over-the-counter (that is not on public exchanges), making the total market unfathomable. A concern must be that the risk models that underlie these derivative positions do not adequately account for the threat of a serious discontinuity in bond and interest rate markets that could occur if there is a fairly rapid rise in inflation expectations, putting the whole financial system under threat.

Investors will probably ultimately find slightly more safety in equities, particularly those that have a clear 'inflation-hedge' characteristic, such as the equity of companies involved in resources. Investments in financial companies should be avoided. The most important thing for anyone who has savings that they do not want to lose is not to be distracted by the siren calls of the investment industry and much of the financial media, who are only too ready to put each decline in markets down to specific events, such as September 11th, or the problems of Enron or WorldCom, or war with Iraq, thereby obscuring this 'big picture'. This is not a conspiracy. It is simply that the nature of the industry, and the symbiosis between the financial institutions and the media, demands that relatively short-term movements in markets have an explanation in the news background of the day, whether that be corporate issues, economics or politics. It is a short step from this to most participants actually believing that the identified issues really are the cause of the markets' behaviour. Some investors then act accordingly, thereby seeming to confirm, for a time, the importance for the markets of these specific issues on which the media concentrates. However, this is all short-term noise. Financial markets and the dollar are in a downtrend and gold, increasingly, appears in an uptrend because of the legacy of the bubble.

From a 'contrarian' perspective there is no real sense that the major financial adjustment has yet taken place, in turn suggesting that the period of poor returns from equity markets is still far from over. At the end of 2002, the main professional players in the financial markets – the strategists and analysts at the big investment companies and investment banks – are still trying to 'pick the bottom' in the stock market, as they have been doing since October 2000. At that time a Reuters news agency report headed 'Investors See Bull Run' (13 October 2000) quoted a number of chief investment officers and heads of asset allocation at major asset managers with comments such as 'I wouldn't like to guess the bottom but I think we are quite near a turning point', and 'With ... markets looking oversold it is a good time for medium to long-term investors to accumulate.' It was the same story in the spring of 2001. In April of that year a similar news agency report talked of a 'growing chorus of fund managers and strategists' making the case for a return to stocks. This was not the last time that the professional investment community has called the market bottom in this bear market, and no doubt there will be more.

The US stock market bubble was absolutely massive in scope, as has been emphasized in this book. This is something which everyone knows, yet at the same time somehow seems easily forgotten now. Viewers of financial channel CNBC in the late 1990s saw a constant stream of fund managers recommending to them the stocks of high-tech darlings such as Cisco Systems and JDS Uniphase. For a long while, viewers taking the advice received instant gratification, as these stocks went up virtually day after day, week after week, month after month. The market seemed impervious to bad news. When, in November 1999, the judge in the antitrust case against Microsoft found against the company in a 'universally negative' legal finding, the stock market treated it as good news and went sharply higher. The reasons given by analysts ranged from the ruling being good for competitors, to the fact that it made it more likely that the company would seek an early settlement. As one chief investment strategist put it at the time, 'Wall Street is viewing this as a buying opportunity.' At the peak of the bubble all news was good news and good news was fantastic news. A bear market is the gradual replacement of this type of sentiment with disillusionment, and this process has been taking a long time to occur. It certainly had not even begun by 5 December 2000 when the NASDAQ index scored its biggest ever gain, rising by 10.5 per cent in a single day, to the widespread acclaim of market commentators. While individual companies might again perform as well in the future for specific reasons, the technology stocks collectively will not, not for a long time.

The investment environment is undergoing a seachange, whatever the perspective of what lies on the other side of the unfolding financial and economic adjustment. Yet the sense at the moment is that professional investors are still clinging to the notions that made them money in the 1990s. This can be seen in the fact that the US stock market retains its relative out-performance of the European markets even though it was the US stock market that was at the centre of the global financial bubble. It can also be seen in the slow rate of downward adjustment of the US dollar, and in market phenomena such as investors' lack of enthusiasm for gold and precious metal stocks despite the uptrend in the underlying metals prices. All these features of markets at the end of 2002 and beginning of 2003 reflect the fact that professional investors are still preferring to believe that the falls in equity prices have happened because of specific one-off events. They stubbornly refuse to recognize that a major secular shift is taking place, and continue to believe that it is only a matter of time before things are back as they were. As long as this remains the underlying sentiment, it merely provides further confirmation that the necessary adjustment has not yet taken place and that markets will fall further.

'Back to Basics'

The new millennium seems likely to have seen the beginning of a new era in financial markets, very different from that of the 1990s. The investment rules that investors learned in the 1990s will have to be unlearned. The economic forces that the financial industry, and the corporate sector in general, have to contend with will be different. Much of the global financial structure that exists today, including the financial companies that comprise it, the people who work for those companies and their investment philosophies and beliefs, as well as the financial instruments that are traded, will probably in the end prove to have been more dependent upon the financial bubble environment than could have been imagined. In the investment world, and contrary to some opinion, the rapid growth of hedge funds in very recent years is probably already an early pointer to a long-term future in which the investment institutions will again be smaller, more specialized, and be required to pay attention to measures of risk and return that are relevant to clients' long-term needs and the structure of their liabilities, rather than to performance measured simply relative to market indices. This is not to ignore the fact that many of today's hedge funds would be unlikely to survive the transition to a higher inflation regime and the financial disruption that will accompany it.

Investment analysis, both corporate and macro-strategy, is also likely in future to have more fundamental depth and add value to the investment process such that it becomes worth fund managers' while to pay for it, either directly or via business relationships. The bull market reduced much (although certainly not all) research to superficial comment distributed in large volumes and fairly indiscriminately by the investment banks. As veteran Wall Street economist Henry Kaufman has remarked,

'The greatest weakness of current reports is their almost complete concentration on the profit-and-loss statement – and failure to analyse balance sheets in any depth. Most research reports fail to probe fundamental issues such as the corporation's liquidity and borrowing capacity; the adequacy of its lines of credit; the likelihood of a change of credit ratings on new or outstanding bond issues; and the contingent liabilities reflected in footnotes.'[21]

Reforms to the US securities industry being proposed to address the issue of conflicts of interest facing analysts working for the investment banks involve the setting up of independent research operations subsidized by these banks. This would be a rather artificial structure for the industry to adopt. In the long run, the forces of market competition ought to work to ensure that research adds value to the investment process and is independent and objective. The problem has been that the rising tide of the bull market lifted nearly all boats and the business of the investment companies became one merely of 'selling product' and not genuinely of doing investment. In that environment, investment research of all types ceased to create much of a competitive advantage and became simply part of the general marketing and sales effort.

On 23 March 1999 Reuters ran a report entitled 'Is the Annual Report Heading for the Bin?' The gist of this article was that in an era when the value of companies supposedly resides in intangible assets such as intellectual property and brand names, the conventional way of valuing companies was 'breaking down' and old-fashioned annual reports no longer did the job of telling investors what the company was worth. Clearly, a few years is a long time in financial markets because the much greater attention paid to accounting practices since the stock market bubble began to burst, and the record pace of restatements of financial accounts by US companies in 2002, suggests that investors and companies have now reverted to a more 'old-fashioned' view of what constitutes a company's value. The tougher financial environment that we face over coming years will tend to re-focus investors and the markets on traditional concepts such as net asset values and dividends. It will also tend to reduce the pressures towards fuzzy concepts such as 'accountability to stakeholders' and 'corporate social responsibility'. These are luxuries that simply cannot be afforded in harsher times, when companies will need to put all their efforts into satisfying shareholders that the fundamentals are sound. Genuine fundamentals will require sound analysis.

The biggest loser in the credibility stakes, however, will probably be the institution of central banking. It is probably inevitable that there will be a fair amount of historical revisionism with respect to the performance of central banks in the 1990s. Where there was once a perception of central banks' (particularly the Fed's) near-infallibility, in future there will be a much greater degree of scepticism with regard to central banks' powers, as it becomes clearer to all that, far from guiding the world economy into an economic miracle, they in fact presided over the creation of a giant financial and economic bubble. The ultimate inability of the central banks to prevent the great destruction of financial wealth that the unwinding of the bubble will bring will heighten this scepticism. Whether or not this will extend to governments seeking to exert more control over central banks, in the guise of making them more accountable, remains to be seen. But it will certainly mean a loss of confidence in central banks' ability to manage the economy to the precise extent that has come to be expected of them. The days when the Bank of England will be considered to be 'missing its inflation target' when it is all of a half per cent from its central expectation will be a thing of the past. Economic management could never be that precise a science, and a healthy dose of scepticism that will come from the widespread acknowledgement of that fact can ultimately only be for the good.

Of course, nobody can genuinely know the future, and even for developments that seem likely to occur, in the case of financial markets nobody can know the exact timing. However, it is possible to make certain useful generalizations that follow from the recognition of the bubble. One is that, in the wake of a bubble the scale of which is unprecedented in history, all financial precedents should be ignored. Claims such as 'the markets cannot go down for another year because this has never happened before' and so on are worthless. Another is that financial developments could quickly move beyond the control of the authorities. Assertions of the type 'inflation cannot rise because central banks have inflation targets and they would not allow it' should also be ignored. If it is the stability of the global financial system that is threatened, then this will take precedence over inflation targets. Investors would be wise to focus on the messages emanating from the medium-to-longer-term trends in the financial markets, particularly the gold and commodities markets, and the foreign exchange markets. One thing that is certain is that the greatest financial bubble the world has ever seen will take a long time to play out fully.

References and Bibliography

1. Charles P. Kindleberger, *Manias, Panics, and Crashes – A History of Financial Crises*, 4th edn (John Wiley & Sons, 2000), pp.2–7.
2. Paul Ormerod, *Butterfly Economics* (Faber & Faber, 1998), pp.1–10.
3. George Soros, *The Alchemy of Finance* (John Wiley & Sons, 1987,1994).
4. Anthony B. Perkins and Michael C. Perkins, *The Internet Bubble – Inside the Overvalued World of High-Tech Stocks and What You Need to Know to Avoid the Coming Shakeout* (HarperBusiness, 1999).
5. Robert J. Shiller, *Irrational Exuberance* (Princeton University Press, 2000).
6. Barton M. Biggs, 'Groupstink', *Morgan Stanley Dean Witter Strategy and Economics* (5 April 1999).
7. Robert J. Gordon, 'Has the "New Economy" Rendered the Productivity Slowdown Obsolete?', *Northwestern University and NBER* (14 June 1999).
8. Edward Chancellor, *Devil Take the Hindmost: A History of Financial Speculation* (Farrar Straus & Giroux, 1999; Palgrave Macmillan, 2000).
9. Tim Lee, 'The Impact of Monetary Policies on World Markets', *The LGT Guide to World Equity Markets 1997* (Euromoney Publications, 1997), p.10.
10. John Montgomery, 'The Acceleration of Global Money Supplies', *Morgan Stanley Dean Witter Economics* (24 March 1999).
11. Stephen Roach, 'Getting Policy Right', *Morgan Stanley Dean Witter Global Economics* (18 June 1999).
12. Andrew Smithers and Stephen Wright, *Valuing Wall Street – Protecting Wealth in Turbulent Markets* (McGraw-Hill, 2000).
13. Benjamin Graham and David Dodd, *Security Analysis – The Classic 1934 Edition* (McGraw-Hill), pp.452–5.
14. Peter Warburton, *Debt and Delusion – Central Bank Follies That Threaten Economic Disaster* (Allen Lane/The Penguin Press, 1999).
15. Tony Jackson, 'Investors Play the Blame Game', *Financial Times* (9 November 2002).
16. Daniel Murray, 'Employee Stock Options: The Fed Joins In', *Smithers and Co. Report No.142* (20 January 2000).
17. Byron R. Wien, 'The Beginning of History', *Morgan Stanley Dean Witter US Investment Research* (7 February 2000).
18. Barry Riley, 'Curse of Benchmarking', *Financial Times* (24 March 1999).
19. E. Crooks and P. Despeignes, 'View from Afar: US Uncritical but Britain Sees Room for Improvement', *Financial Times* (20 December 2001).
20. Graham and Dodd, *Security Analysis*, pp.14–15.
21. Henry Kaufman, 'A Straighter Path for Wall Street', *Financial Times* (4 December 2002).

Index